CRUSH MATH NOW

High-Impact Strategies for Students Who Struggle with Math

ALLISON DILLARD

Happy Hypotenuse Publishing, LLC

For my Prealgebra students,

A Calculus student
is just a
Prealgebra student
who
never gave up.

—

And for my husband Joe,

Every day,
my love for you grows
exponentially.

SPECIAL INVITATION

Crush Math Now for Students: I've created *free* resources to help you crush math! If additional guidance and motivation will help you jump from struggling with math to crushing it, please join www.crushmathnow.com/students and I'll help you every step of the way.

Crush Math Now for Educators: It takes a village to empower a student to succeed in math. If you are an educator, who wants to learn high-impact teaching strategies, please join www.crushmathnow.com/educators. We'd love for you to join our village!

CONTENTS

INTRODUCTION

If you're anything like my students, you want to improve your math grade as drastically, efficiently, and quickly as humanly possible. So let's get to it. You've got a problem (math), a deadline (your next quiz or test), and you need someone to help you solve your problem. Hence, this book: *Crush Math Now*. What exactly do I mean when I say I want you to crush math now?

Crush because I don't want you to use this book to timidly scrape by in math, pass just barely or by pure luck, and end your class just as timid and unconfident as you are today. When you finish with this book, I want you to have CRUSHED MATH. I want you to walk away feeling powerful. I want you to have the confidence that you can do anything, that you can solve any problem, that you can overcome any challenge. In your quest to become the kind of person you will be proud of, this book will help you figure out how to crush math, which in turn will give you the power to do the things you think you cannot do.

Math because that's the challenge you're faced with today. Math is likely the scary, stressful requirement that stands between where you are now and your dream college, major, or career. To be worthy of those dreams, you must become the kind of person who can crush whatever is required of you, including math. It's more than that, though. Just as sports and working out exercise and strengthen your muscles, learning math strengthens your mind, your problem-solving skills, and your ability to find patterns and make inferences. It is the Olympics of mental strength, stamina, and ability. Yes, math is hard. It won't get easier, either. This book will help you become awesome at it, though.

Now because you can't change what happened in the past, and you have no control over what you'll face in the future. Future You (you know, "you," but six hours or two weeks from now) isn't dependable. Future You not only easily gets tired, distracted, and frustrated but can "accidentally" spend two hours on Instagram. You can't control Future You (whom I will refer to throughout the book). You can, however, control what you do *now*. Right *now*, you are to do the following: Finish the introduction and read Chapter 1.

That's it. Don't worry about anything else. Just focus on what you can do right now.

WHY YOU MUST CRUSH MATH

As a college freshman, in my own personal quest to make the most out of college, I asked college seniors, "If you could do college over again, what would you do differently?" I always got one of two answers. Half responded, "I wish I would've had more fun," and the other half said, "I wish I would have studied more." So I went through college determined to balance the two. I was determined to one day look back at my college years without regret—to be able to say, "If I had to do college over, I'd do it exactly the same!"

Here's the thing: Nobody looks back at high school or college and wishes they'd failed math. Or stressed out more. Or procrastinated more. Or let their stupid, boring math requirement consume their life, only to fall short of their goals. Math, I believe, is a problem that prevents many students from making the most of high school and college. If you ignore it and focus on having fun, you'll look back and wish you'd tried harder. If you let your math scores consume your life, on the other hand, you'll miss out on the fun side of high school and college. There's a balance that can be struck. This is why I want to teach you how to crush math. Quickly. Effectively. Confidently. No matter how alien math feels to you, no matter how much you hate, fear, or dread it, at the end of this process, you will look back at high school and college and say that you not only passed math, you *crushed* it.

MEET COACH ALLISON

Hi! I'm Coach Allison. Technically, I'm a math professor, not a coach, but I like the title coach better. It reminds me that I need to challenge you and I need to keep it interesting. I need to give you a reason to show up every day and work hard. It also reminds you, the student, that you are in charge of your future. Your success is not determined by your coach; as in any sport, it's the work that you, the individual, put in that will decide whether or not you succeed. I will not baby you or pity you or hold your hand as you complain about anything that's standing in the way of you succeeding in math. As your coach, I will tell you to toughen up and figure out a way to overcome the obstacle. Sound good?

In addition to being your coach, I am also an optimist who believes that anyone can crush math. Why do I believe this? Because I've seen it happen over and over and over again. Before I was a math professor, I spent nearly two decades working as a math tutor. From high school until my early-thirties, the one constant in my life was helping students, day in and day out, to crush math. I helped failing students pass, passing students get A's, and A students maintain their grades in a quarter of the time. I helped students who hated or were terrified of math to thrive and gain confidence. I helped unmotivated students get motivated. I helped students who were distracted by everything under the sun learn to focus and develop discipline. I helped students find strategies to crush obstacles like dyslexia, ADHD, math anxiety, and this nonsensical notion of "not being a math person." I helped students turn everything around over a weekend, optimize their studying in a month, and go on to take classes and reach goals they never imagined at the beginning.

Over the years, I got to the point where I'd seen so many struggling students catapult their grades and surpass their goals that I came to believe that *anyone* can crush math. This is still what I believe today.

Anyone can crush math.

Today, as a math professor, I have the advantage of seeing which students succeed and which don't, what qualities encapsulate students who will beat the odds and what qualities characterize students who will fail. As someone who spent decades working one-on-one with the students who were most likely to fail and helping them succeed, my heart always goes out to the underdogs. The ones who give up too easily. The ones who are stuck in a rut, continually approaching math in a way that isn't working. The ones who want to succeed but just can't figure out how. My heart goes out to them because I know that with the right changes, they can do it. I know that anyone can crush math—if they only know how.

If you don't believe me right now, that's fine. Let's not worry too much about who you'll be at the end of this book. Let's just focus on stuff that will help you today, like a quick crash course in the three steps you must take to crush math.

THE CRUSH MATH NOW FORMULA

The Crush Math Now Formula boils down to three steps:

1. **Identify Your Problems**. Emphasis on the "s" in problems. As soon as you get beyond generalizations, like "I hate math" or "I'm no good at math" or "my math teacher is bad," you'll find very specific problems with very specific solutions.
2. **Crush Your Problems**. You'll do this by experimenting, trying the different solutions I provide in this book, and thinking outside the box to come up with your own solutions. The focus here is to change what you're doing.
3. **Optimize What You're Doing**. To do anything well, you must repeatedly review and analyze what you're doing. Keep strategies that are high-impact. Cut strategies that aren't. Then, tweak or refine the things that aren't quite working, but have potential.

That's it! The beauty of the Crush Math Now Formula is that it's simple and easy to follow. The individual steps, however, require some honest self-analysis on your part, along with some hard work. (Sorry, there's no getting around that.) That means, first and foremost, discovering your biggest math problems so you can overcome them.

TURNING MATH PROBLEMS INTO SOLUTIONS

Even I—your math-loving, math-conquering coach—can see that a lot of things about math can, in fact, suck. It can be boring. It can be hard. It doesn't always relate to real life. It can have too many rules. Too many steps. Too many ever-so-slightly different problems with ever-so-slightly different steps. In the worst of cases, math can simply be an ever-changing, soul-crushing academic requirement that slowly, methodically, and painfully sucks the happiness from your life and leaves you stressed and insecure.

The actual problems that stand between where you are now in math and where you want to be are vast and varied. Before we get into those problems, I want to recommend that you adopt a habit I have developed in dealing with problems. I rewrite problems in the form of questions. Why? Because it empowers you and helps you focus on finding a solution.

For example, far and away the most common problem students have is thinking "I'm not good at math." I would rewrite this as, "How do I become good at math?" If your problem is dyslexia, write: "How do I overcome dyslexia to succeed in math?" Rewriting problems as questions reminds you that problems are just questions that need solutions. Like in life, some of your math problems are harder to solve than others, but ultimately they all have solutions.

Here are a few of the most common problems with math, in the form of questions:

- How do I succeed if I'm not a math person?
- How can I become motivated enough to study and do my homework?
- How can I succeed when I hate math?
- How can I succeed if math terrifies me?

- How can I succeed if I've failed math before?
- How can I succeed if I can't finish tests on time?
- How can I succeed if I make many careless errors on tests?
- How can I succeed if I forget formulas and definitions on tests?
- How can I succeed if I blank out on steps that I can do in homework?
- How can I succeed if I have panic attacks during tests?
- How do I overcome dyslexia to succeed in math?
- How do I overcome ADHD to succeed in math?
- How do I overcome math anxiety?
- How do I overcome multiple learning disorders?
- How can I succeed if I do all the work and study all the time but am still failing my tests?
- How do I cram if my test is tomorrow?
- How do I balance sports, extracurriculars, and math?
- How do I balance work, raising a family, and math?
- How do I succeed if I have a bad teacher?
- How do I succeed if class is a waste of time?
- How do I succeed if my class doesn't even have a textbook?

In addition to the common questions above, as a tutor, I discovered that there are also certain questions that students *never* ask, which are just as crucial to raising their math grades. These questions may not have direct solutions linked to them, but they get to the roots of problems, which are just as crucial as "how to" steps. These include:

- Why do I fear math?

- Why do I think I'm not a math person?
- Why do I hate math?
- Why am I unmotivated?
- Why do I need to succeed in math?

These important *why* questions are also discussed and answered in this book.

HOW THE BOOK WORKS

In structuring *Crush Math Now*, I felt it was important to take into consideration your limited time. As such, I've broken the book down so that you don't need to read the whole book but rather can do some initial analysis, identify what your particular problems are, and then jump to the sections that will help you the most.

The only required chapters are "Chapter 1: The Crush Math Now Formula," "Chapter 2: Problems, Goals, and Game Plans," and "Chapter 11: Optimize What You're Doing." For everything in between, pick and choose what's most relevant to you.

Chapter 1: The Crush Math Now Formula walks you through the formula's successful application by three real students. The first student, Priscilla, had a strong work ethic but had failed Precalculus three times and developed such severe math anxiety that she had panic attacks during tests. The second student, Harper, simply hated math more than anything and couldn't bring herself to do the work. Procrastination alone, literally, was causing her to fail. The third student, Dylan, had a learning disability. Though he had tried everything under the sun, he couldn't figure out how *not* to make mistakes on his tests.

Chapter 2: Problems, Goals and Game Plans guides

you through the first step in the Crush Math Now Formula by helping you to more specifically identify your problems. You'll break down your problems with math in terms of the specific grades you need, your competency or understanding of the material you're expected to know, and your underlying problems.

Chapters 3-7 provide solutions to the underlying problems that are impacting your math grade. These changes will not just improve how you approach math but will enable you to approach anything with confidence.

Chapter 3: What to Do If You Procrastinate or Lack Motivation—If you procrastinate on homework and studying, end up cramming the night before your math test, and don't study enough, your math grade suffers. Maybe you also struggle to show up to class. Maybe you also don't do the homework. Maybe you don't care enough to ask for help. Even if you are totally on top of other areas of your life, you just can't focus on math and get the work done. If this is you, read this chapter first. None of the other chapters will help you if you don't have the motivation to see it through.

Chapter 4: What to Do If You Have Math Anxiety or Lack Confidence—If you lack confidence, you need to study and prepare for exams in a way that teaches you the material well enough and builds your confidence, so your score reflects what you know. Whether you simply blank out or you have full-blown panic attacks and math PTSD, there are strategies to prepare better and overcome this.

Chapter 5: What to Do If You Lack Grit and Discipline—You're motivated. Crushing math is important to you. You have confidence. You know that if you actually did the work you know you need to do, you'd crush math. Whether your lack of discipline stems from procrastination, laziness, or simply a lack of focus because everything under the sun is more interesting than math, you need to make a few changes to develop discipline in order to crush math.

Chapter 6: What to Do If You're Struggling to Succeed on Your Own—Maybe you're a student with no family to help out, no school connections, and no friends who've crushed math, and you're doing this alone. Or maybe asking for help is just the last thing you want to do. If you're feeling isolated and alone in this journey and don't know how or where to reach out for help, this chapter will help you. Here's the honest truth: It takes a village to crush math, and it takes a village to be successful in life. This chapter will show you how to build that village from the ground up and get the support you need.

Chapter 7: What to Do If You Have an Emergency or Permanent Obstacle—Everyone has problems. Life would be boring without them. However, when your problems get in the way of crushing math, they must be dealt with ASAP. If you have a learning disability, English is your second language, you have kids, you work full-time, or you are an adult returning to school, this chapter addresses problems specific to your situation. Indecisiveness and inaction are your greatest enemies here. Let's figure out a plan to crush your problems so you have the ability to crush math.

Once you've crushed the underlying problems, Chapters 8-10 walk you through more tactical solutions to raising your grades.

Chapter 8: What to Do If You Study Ineffectively or Just Don't Understand Math—If you study all the time but are still struggling, then what you are doing isn't working. This chapter will help you pinpoint the problems with how you study. (Hint: Reviewing notes does not count as studying.) It will teach you to complete homework in such a way that you are simultaneously studying for your exams. This, in turn, allows for deeper, more specific studying the night before your exam.

Chapter 9: What to Do If You Study and Take Test Too Slowly— Some people may tell you it's okay to trudge through math at a snail's pace, understanding it, but going through slowly and meticulously. However, if this is impacting your grade because you don't finish tests on time, you must pick up the pace. You need strategies that help you focus, study and take tests more efficiently. Note: This chapter is also helpful if you're over-scheduled and just want to sprint through math.

Chapter 10: What to Do if You're Failing or Doing Poorly on Tests—Students who feel they have poor test-taking skills typically have weak foundations and study ineffectively. Read Chapter 8 first, then come back to Chapter 10, which focuses on strategies for the morning of, right before, and during your exam. This chapter covers every hack, tip, and strategy I know for recalling important information, reducing careless errors, and gaining the most points on tests, but you must study first.

The last chapter provides you with tools to help you through your initial challenge of crushing math.

Chapter 11: Optimize What You're Doing walks you through how to improve what you're doing. By identifying your problems and trying out the most relevant solutions, you're making an educated guess, rather than just going by trial and error. Educated guesses, however, are not always correct. In most cases, you'll see some improvement but will need to make additional changes as you go. Chapter 11 provides you with exercises that will help you to review and analyze the changes you've made so you can keep the most high-impact strategies, cut anything that's low-impact, and tweak strategies that seem promising but aren't producing results as you had hoped. Through this process, you will be able to dig deep enough to find the changes that will catapult your grade so you can achieve your goals.

FIVE RULES TO MAKE THE MOST OF CRUSH MATH NOW

To get the most out of this book, I recommend the following:

1. Focus on change. If you don't like the results you're getting in your math class, you must change what you're doing. If you're not putting in the time, put in the time. If your foundations are weak, but you've been carrying on despite that—go back and strengthen your foundations. If you bombed your last test, change how you study for the next one. If you want different results in your math class, you must change how you study math, how you think about math, how you schedule math, how you do everything related to math. In fact, if you want different results in any area of your life, you must change what you're doing. As the internet claims Albert Einstein once said, "Insanity is doing the same thing over and over again and expecting different results."

2. Don't read the whole book. Just as you should never read your math textbook cover to cover, you also do not need to read this book cover to cover. In classes, you read what your teacher tells you is important or what you intuitively think will be important. As your coach, I'm telling you that Chapters 1, 2, and 11 are important for everyone, so be sure to read those.

Beyond that, use your judgment. Trust your intuition. Read the chapters that you think will have the most impact on your grade, and work on strengthening those skills. (The 80/20 rule, discussed in depth in Chapter 9, says that if you try many different things—because this principle pertains to big numbers—80 percent of your results will come from 20 percent of the things you do. As such, 80 percent of your grade improvement will come from 20 percent of the solutions in this book.) Try lots of different things in this book and look for the few that will make the biggest impact on your grade.

3. Accept responsibility. There is no fairy godmother who will appear, wave a magic wand, and make math easy. Realize that whether or not you crush math is all on you—on the actions you take, on the changes you make, and on the work you put in.

Let's assume you're in the worst-case scenario: You're in a math class you're unqualified to be in. You've failed it before and, rightfully so, have zero confidence. Your homework is too hard or confusing, and you know deep in your heart that you're 100 percent not prepared for your next exam. You hate math —understandably so in this situation—and are therefore a procrastinator. Your teacher is unsympathetic, unhelpful, and incompetent. You have no support system. You have a learning disorder, and you're also going through a personal crisis, such as being homeless, battling depression, or dealing with a medical emergency. Yes, I think that qualifies as a worst-case scenario.

As hard as it sounds, you need to accept your situation for what it is: a challenge. An obstacle that needs to be overcome. A problem to be solved. Decide whether you want to solve it and, if you do, commit to it. Accept 100 percent responsibility for your own success. Whatever happens, be able to look back and say you gave it 100 percent of your effort.

As Martin Luther King Jr. once said, "The ultimate measure of a man is not where he stands in moments of comfort and convenience, but where he stands at times of challenge."

4. Do the "Crush Math Now" exercises. You must do the exercises throughout this book. This is the difference between hiring a private tutor who is guaranteed to improve your grade versus reading a book, which may or may not. If I was your math tutor, I would *make* you do these exercises. I'd be sitting right there next to you, waiting for you to answer the questions. With a book, however, you must have the self-discipline to do the exercises when no one is looking over your shoulder. To actually crush math, do the "Crush Math Now" exercises.

5. Enjoy it. Even if you can't get excited about math itself, at least get excited about the person you're becoming as you learn to crush math. While, yes, your goals will be focused on grades and perhaps a subject you're less than thrilled with, you'll learn so much more.

You'll learn how to set goals and develop the discipline to follow through with them. You'll learn how to take those feelings of hopelessness and powerlessness and flip them around so that you're in control and you decide what's going to happen. You'll learn how to motivate yourself. Can you imagine living in a world where motivation isn't some magical, fleeting thing that comes and goes but something you have control over?

Yes, you'll learn hacks to catch your mistakes on exams or study faster, but most importantly you'll become the kind of person who can do the thing they think they cannot do. Enjoy it.

IMAGINE FUTURE YOU

Imagine you are awesome at math. You blaze through homework in record time, rock your exams, and love the rush you get upon solving a crazy hard problem.

Imagine you love math. You feel confident in your ability to learn new things, your ability to solve problems, and your ability to overcome challenges.

Imagine you have the skills, confidence, and grit necessary to succeed in any type of math, as well as anything in life. The sky's the limit now. How would that change Future You? How would it change your goals and your future?

I know you're reading this book to solve a problem. Your math grade is the problem, and I am the expert here to help you solve the problem. I must admit, however, that I wrote this book with an ulterior motive. You see, unlike many people, I love math. I believe that math empowers students. It teaches them to solve problems and conquer challenges. It develops within them grit and confidence. It enables them to figure out how to do the things they think they cannot do so that they can live bigger, bolder, more inspired lives.

My hope is that you will not just crush math but that you will learn to love it. Why? Because in return, math will help you become anything you ever dreamed of being. Be a bartender who loves math. Be a screenwriter who loves math. Be a soccer player who plays beer pong and loves math. Be a fitness instructor who runs on the beach every morning and loves math. I have been all these things, and each was better because I loved math.

Life is short, and I encourage you to go that extra mile and be the best that you can be. And the best version of yourself, no matter who you are, is someone capable of crushing math.

CRUSH MATH NOW

Imagine Future You. You're crushing math. You consistently get A's and you're confident that with enough effort and ingenuity you can figure out any difficult math problem your teacher throws at you.

Get a piece of paper and set a timer for five minutes. Write down as many details as you can about Future You. How will you be different? How will you feel about yourself? How will others view you? What will your daily approach to math be? What habits will you have formed? What skills will you have gained? What new bigger, bolder dreams might you be pursuing? Write for five minutes. Go!

1. THE CRUSH MATH NOW FORMULA

If you're reading this book, you want to crush math but don't know how, and the basic study guides that accompany math courses rarely tap the surface of what you need. To crush math, you must understand that there is no one-size-fits-all solution. Just as there is no universal diet plan, road to wealth, or dress size, there is also no single road to success in math. Every student who makes the leap from struggling to getting an A must identify the specific problems that are holding them back, try out solutions, and find the answers that work for them and their situation.

To get started, I want you to see how the Crush Math Now Formula worked for three students, so you know what to expect as you do this on your own. There are three steps to the Crush Math Now Formula:

Step 1: Identify Your Problems. One student might hate math and lack the motivation to buckle down and do the work. Another student might have poor test-taking skills and be plagued with test anxiety. And yet another student might struggle simply because they over-scheduled themselves, got sick, or fell behind. The problems are different for everyone, and you must identify your specific problems.

Step 2: Crush Your Problems. Once you've identified your problems, your next job is to read through many different solutions, identify those that you think will make the biggest difference in your grade, and try them.

Remember: If you want different results in your math class, you must change how you do math. Try out the things that you think will have the largest impact on your grade. In this step, you must focus on changing what you're doing, as you work to replace how you previously did things with something better. I'll give you a heads up now. This will require trying new things and going out of your comfort zone.

Step 3: Optimize What You're Doing. Reflect. Think about the new strategies you tried. What worked? What didn't? Keep what's working and change what's not. What problems were fixed? What problems remain? Celebrate the wins and find new solutions for the problems that remain. Keep the things that are making a big impact and cut what's not. Tweak or customize the things that have potential to help but could be better.

In this step, you must focus on honesty and consistency. If you don't reflect honestly, you'll just make excuses, fall into the passive mindset that succeeding in math is out of your control, and fail to make the changes you must make in order to succeed. If you don't reflect consistently, your progress will stagnate. Remember: 20 percent of the solutions in this book will yield 80 percent of your grade improvement. It's up to you to reflect on your changes and find the 20 percent of solutions that will catapult you to an A in math.

MEET HARPER, PRISCILLA, AND DYLAN

The three steps of the Crush Math Now Formula are best illustrated with examples, so let me introduce you to Harper, Priscilla, and Dylan.

Harper had no confidence and no *math* work ethic. (Note: I say *math* work ethic because students can have an incredible work ethic in other areas of their lives, but not in math. This was the case for Harper.) Self-proclaimed as "not a math person," Harper was highly involved with her high school theater productions, enjoyed surfing, and socialized exclusively with other "not math" people. She not only procrastinated on getting help until she was failing high school Algebra II but also blamed everything else for her math struggles: her teacher, the textbook, her homework, the tests, her tutors, her parents, and the subject itself. You name it, and she'd probably cast blame on it. What made this even worse was that procrastinating didn't remove the stress of failing math; It simply followed her around everywhere, trying oh-so-hard to ruin her life.

Priscilla, on the other hand, had an incredible math work ethic but no confidence. A college junior who had failed Precalculus twice and withdrawn a third time, Priscilla had severe math anxiety. It had grown to the point that she had panic attacks during her math exams, and you can't pass math if you cry, hyperventilate, and think you're having a heart attack during your final. You just can't.

Dylan had both confidence and a strong math work ethic but still wasn't succeeding. As a student with severe dyslexia, he couldn't raise his SAT Math score above 400, despite knowing that his math skill level was 600+. He'd worked with multiple test prep companies and tutors to no avail, and, if he couldn't figure out how to raise his score, he wouldn't get into the college he knew he was qualified to attend.

I wanted to introduce you to Harper, Priscilla, and Dylan because, although their problems are very personal and specific to them, they do highlight some of the common strengths and weaknesses that many struggling math students have. Therefore, learning from their journeys may help you to kickstart yours. Harper had no confidence and no math work ethic. Priscilla had a strong work ethic and studied all the time, but she had zero confidence. Dylan had confidence and a strong work ethic, yet he still struggled.

Let's look at how the Crush Math Now Formula helped them to crush math.

STEP 1: IDENTIFY YOUR PROBLEMS.

Your problems are often not what you think, so this is something you need to reassess constantly.

Harper thought her problems were bad teachers, hard homework, and questions with too many confusing steps. These were just excuses, though. Her problem was needing to change the deeply rooted mindset that she was "not a math person" and the common consequence of that: procrastination.

Priscilla thought her problem was "not being a math person" and having math anxiety, but these were consequences of having failed. Her actual problem was studying incorrectly. She'd spent semesters failing because she passively reviewed her notes and read her book to study for exams. For her, this clearly wasn't working, and drastic changes to her study habits needed to be made.

Dylan thought his problem was making mistakes due to dyslexia. While that was partially true, he'd forgotten the second part to that: catching his mistakes. To crush a math test, you only need to solve one of those two problems. Dylan's secondary problem was that he didn't know as much as he thought and therefore was making legitimate mistakes that were being blamed on dyslexia.

STEP 2: CRUSH YOUR PROBLEMS.

The way Harper, Priscilla, and Dylan crushed their problems was through something they were either hesitant to try or had never thought to try. After all, if the solutions were obvious, they wouldn't have found themselves in this predicament. They found what worked by experimenting and focusing on change.

Harper worked through a barrage of different identity and mindset issues. Once her mindset was in the right place, she focused almost exclusively on strategies to study faster (she was highly motivated to spend as little time on math as possible!).

Priscilla focused on first trying different study strategies, then different test-taking and confidence-building strategies.

Dylan studied his various mistakes to see which would be easier to prevent or catch. He also tried new test-taking strategies and, more importantly, strategies for catching errors.

What was the one thing that allowed these students to ultimately succeed? They focused on change. As a tutor and teacher, it seems so obvious, but perhaps not so much for you as a student. Know this: If what you're doing isn't giving you the results you want, then change what you're doing. If you're not getting the grade you want in your math class, then change what you're doing to get it.

STEP 3: OPTIMIZE WHAT YOU'RE DOING

For Harper, Priscilla, and Dylan to quickly find what would raise their grades, they needed to quickly eliminate what *didn't* work. They didn't have a year or even a month to make gradual steps toward optimization. They needed fast results, so they needed to try and assess things quickly. *Step 3: Optimize What You're Doing* looks like this:

1. Identify Your Problem.
2. Try Different Solutions.
3. Reflect and Improve.

You can make lots of tweaks over the course of a week or weekend. Let's look at the different iterations and tweaks Harper, Priscilla and Dylan made before they optimized what they were doing and crushed math.

HOW HARPER OPTIMIZED

Harper made six changes before she crushed math.

Change 1: She learned from a different teacher (me). Harper started off asking me to explain the math to her, thinking that the problem was her teacher not doing a good job teaching the material. The result: That was not the solution. Her eyes would glaze over. She couldn't listen to me talk about math either.

Change 2: She analyzed her relationship with math. We switched to just talking about math and asking "why" questions, such as: *Why do you think you're bad at math? Why do you hate math? Why are none of your friends good at math? Why do you consider yourself a good surfer?* We also explored what would happen if she took that dedication, perseverance, and willingness to make mistakes from surfing and applied it to math. The result: the first baby step. We discovered several reasons *why* she lacked motivation and confidence in math. First, her parents loved math, and she had a tumultuous relationship with them (understatement of the century). Second, she had no friends who were successful at or encouraging about math. Lastly, she was afraid to try and fail.

Change 3: We zeroed in on motivation. If she could figure out a strong reason *why* she needed to succeed in math, she could find the motivation to try. First, we separated math from her relationship with her parents. (Her parents wanted her to do well, so failing angered them—which was motivating her to fail. That thinking had to be discarded because it was hurting her.) We figured out exactly, in a perfect world, what she aspired to do: what she wanted to major in (theater), where she wanted to go to college (one that required math), and what she wanted to do (run her own theater company). The result: nothing. She still wouldn't try.

Change 4: We zeroed in on *why* she was afraid to try. We talked about learning to surf and the numerous times she fell but picked herself back up again. We talked about acting, how far she'd come from her very first performance, and how she kept on learning, improving, and tweaking her craft. While everyone had perhaps chalked her up to being a "natural actress," it took a lot of hard work to become that way. The plan was to try—with no regard for failing. The result: She finally acknowledged that she needed to try but was still afraid to try.

Change 5: We zeroed in on the rarely articulated social fears. Harper was afraid to try because she had a reputation for being a slacker, and her friends would judge her for trying. Especially if she tried and failed. Therefore, I convinced her to study and try, but not tell anyone. She didn't need to tell her friends. She didn't need to tell her parents. She would do it in complete isolation, so she wouldn't be embarrassed if she failed. The result: She got the highest score in her class on the first math test she actually tried.

Change 6: She went back to studying and test-taking hacks to shorten how long she needed to study. Result: She minimized the amount of time she spent on math, while acing her tests. Her peers viewed her as both a slacker and a math rockstar, and she loved it.

End result: Harper maintained her slacker image and boosted her math grade to the top of the class. She figured out how to sprint through her homework in record time, prepare for exams quickly and efficiently, and free up more time and energy for the things that really mattered to her.

HOW PRISCILLA OPTIMIZED

Priscilla, on the other hand, made six very different changes before she crushed math:

Change 1: Priscilla started off focusing on memorization techniques and test-taking hacks, thinking that if she knew the material more thoroughly, she wouldn't blank out on exams. Result: It didn't translate to solving problems correctly.

Change 2: Priscilla focused on doing practice problems without her book or notes. Result: She could solve an individual problem, as long as she knew what topic or section it was from. She couldn't solve problems if she didn't already know the strategy to use.

Change 3: Priscilla focused on solving questions in a testlike format. I gave her sets of problems that would be on the test, but mixed them up so she didn't know which section they were from. The result: Her confidence in solving individual problems increased, but her confidence in taking exams did not.

Change 4: She took an actual practice quiz to study for her

next quiz. I made my best guess as to what questions would be on her quiz, wrote them out on paper, and had her take the "quiz." Result: She aced the practice quiz but still blanked out on her real quiz. Again, her confidence in math itself increased, but her confidence in taking tests did not. The next exam was near, so this needed to be fixed quickly!

Change 5: Priscilla focused on *in a test-like setting*. She took an official-looking, printed, timed practice test in the library (as close to a real test setting as possible). Result: She aced the practice test, and her confidence went up. She knew the material inside and out. There were no more gaps in her foundations. There was no test question she couldn't answer...but she was terrified. After three failed semesters, she had true math PTSD.

Change 6: Priscilla wanted to take two more practice tests to build her confidence more, so she did. Under normal circumstances, I would say this is overkill, but there's no such thing as overkill when it comes to conquering math anxiety. She thought two more practice tests would make her feel better, so that's what she did. And the result during the real exam? She crushed her Precalculus final exam. She had enough confidence that she didn't panic or blank out, and she even remembered and used the memorization and test-taking hacks she had studied at the very beginning.

End result: She took three practice tests before she passed the first Precalculus exam, but the good news is that she passed! It was a tremendous amount of work, but it was a one-time mountain to climb. After that, she studied more efficiently and only needed one practice test per exam. All the effort and time came upfront when she needed to solve the problem. Once it was solved, studying became easier and faster, and the process went on autopilot.

HOW DYLAN OPTIMIZED

Dylan, in contrast, made changes to combat his dyslexia and raise his SAT Math score.

Change 1: We looked at Dylan's errors. We made a list of all the types of mistakes he made and tallied up how many there were. The result: Not all of his mistakes were due to dyslexia.

Change 2: We strengthened his foundations, particularly in the order of operations and Geometry. End result: an estimated 30-40 additional points on the SAT Math section.

Change 3: Next, we focused on preventing errors caused by dyslexia. Now, there are a million different strategies to help dyslexic students prevent "careless errors," such as writing out *all* your work (even the most obvious), writing in larger handwriting, requesting exams with larger print, blocking out the other problems, and reading with a paper under each line. The strategies are numerous, and, from my experience, their effectiveness is hit or miss. What works for one student might not work for the next. The result: He was still making errors caused by his dyslexia. After wading through dozens of new strategies, the improvement on his test was an estimated 10-20 points (much to his disappointment and frustration).

Change 4: Next, we focused on checking for mistakes. We tried everything, including rewriting word problems, circling likely places for number reversals, checking how numbers are lined up, double-checking work on the calculator, problem-solving without symbols, double-checking what the question is asking for, etc. The result: Dylan gained an estimated 10-20 points. Overall, he'd jumped from barely 400 to the high 400s. It's not terrible progress, but it wasn't enough.

Change 5: We kept trying new strategies for finding and preventing mistakes. We'd hit the point where we'd run out of articles or literature with helpful new suggestions. Anything we came across, we'd already tried. So we began trying a lot of "what if's." The result: We noticed something *really* peculiar. While *I* was checking Dylan's work, he would catch his mistake. Not while *he* was checking it, but while sitting across the table from me and looking at the paper upside down, his mistakes became apparent to him. Weird, right?

Change 6: We had him take the SAT Math section like normal, expecting him to correctly answer about 20 questions out of 58. He'd need to catch errors on 20 more questions to raise his score to 600. After he took the test, he turned it upside down and checked his work. It took him longer, but even with his extended time, he still finished early. The result: He caught more than 20 errors, surpassed his goal of 600, and scored 640 on the SAT Math section.

The final result: He reached the score that would get him into his dream college. He also learned a useful test-taking hack that would help him succeed in his college math classes. He went on to use it in English as well. We discovered that turning the paper upside down forced him to go so slow that he actually caught the mistakes. I've never seen this work with another dyslexic student, but it worked for Dylan. He never would have succeeded if he hadn't kept experimenting and tracking, experimenting and tracking.

THREE SIMPLE STEPS

And that's the Crush Math Now Formula that helped Harper, Priscilla, and Dylan—along with so many other students— crush math. To recap, those steps are:

1. Identify Your Problems.
2. Crush Your Problems.
3. Optimize What You're Doing.

Without those three steps, it's easy to struggle aimlessly or go years without improving how you tackle math. When done correctly, it's so simple and straightforward. The awesome thing about going through this process is that it can help you raise your grade quickly. You can do this over the course of a week or even a weekend. You can make a year's worth of improvements overnight and show up to class a completely different person. Even better—the Crush Math Now Formula can help you not only learn to crush math, but it can also help you to crush anything with which you struggle.

If you read something and think, "I wish I'd done that on my last test!" or "I should totally be doing that," try it out. If your gut reaction is, "that's a waste of time," or "there's no way that would help," don't bother with it. Every student has different preferences and faces different obstacles in their path to success, so every student will require a different combination of solutions to succeed.

CRUSH MATH NOW

The fastest way to improve is to learn from mistakes. Did Harper, Priscilla, or Dylan make any mistakes that you can learn from? Write down any ideas you can use to study for your next quiz or test.

2. PROBLEMS, GOALS AND GAME PLANS

You are not powerless, and your problems are not unsolvable. Problems are just obstacles standing between you and success. Let's identify the obstacles that stand between you and crushing math, then turn them into specific goals with concrete steps you can take toward those goals. Your math "problems" break down into three specific obstacles:

Obstacle 1: Your Grades—You need to know exactly what your current grade is, how many assignments remain, and what grades you must get on your remaining assignments and exams to reach your goals. Your grades determine your goals, along with the milestones you must hit to finish with the grade you want on your report card.

Obstacle 2: Your Competency—You must clarify exactly what you should study to get the grades you need. Your competency levels on different topics will turn into your study to-do list, so you will know exactly what you need to study and when.

Obstacle 3: You—What are your underlying problems? Ultimately, your success doesn't just depend on buckling down and learning the specific homework and test questions you don't know. That's obvious. You must fix the underlying problems, all the non-math stuff that's holding you back. And guess what? That's the same stuff that'll hold you back in other areas of your life. So the good news is that, as you transform yourself into the type of person who can crush math, you'll also turn yourself into the type of person who can crush anything.

If you want to overcome these obstacles, you must first be prepared. Obstacle number one—your grades—will require math to calculate exactly what grades you need to receive on your remaining assignments. Obstacle number two—your competency—will require hard, focused work, which is more mentally exerting than the minimal, mindless homework drills to which math students are accustomed. Obstacle number three—you—will require introspection and honesty to find the underlying problems that most impact your grades. If you've never really analyzed yourself before, that's okay. It's time to practice. After all, you want to develop into a human being who has the ability to assess yourself critically, acknowledge your strengths, admit your weaknesses, and figure out how to develop into a stronger person.

CRUSH MATH NOW

Get out a piece of paper or open up a document on your computer. At the top of the page, write *Crush Math Now Game Plan*. Did you do it? Yes? Awesome! By the end of this chapter, you'll have a rough draft of the game plan that will take you from where you are now to the grade you want. Alright, let's create your *Crush Math Now Game Plan*!

First, let's take a look at each obstacle in more detail.

OBSTACLE 1: YOUR GRADES

Depending on when in the semester or quarter you're reading this, you'll fall into one of three groups:

Beginning of the Semester: This is the ideal place to be! You're starting with a clean slate and this book at your disposal, so you'll tackle this math class differently and better than any math class you've tackled before. At this point, any goal is possible! The sky's the limit. Your goal is an A.

Middle of the Semester: You've turned in some assignments and taken some exams. These grades are already set in stone and will influence your goals. You must calculate what grades you'll need on the remaining assignments to get the final grade you want. These calculations can be tedious, but it's worth it because you'll know exactly what grades you need on which assignments.

End of the Semester: Most of your grades are already set in stone. You must do some math to determine what outcomes are possible and plan accordingly.

If you fall into groups two or three, you must calculate your current grade and assess your remaining assignments to see if an A is possible. If it isn't, adjust your goal accordingly. To do this, you need your graded assignments and your syllabus (or information on how your grades are weighted).

Next, use the average formula or weighted percents to calculate your current grade and calculate the grades you will need on the remaining assignments in order to reach your goal.

If you can work through this quickly, do it now. If you think it'll take too long, ask your parents, your math teacher, or your school's tutoring center to help you figure it out.

Think this step is a waste of time? Sometimes just knowing what you need can crush being overwhelmed and allow you to move forward with confidence. Take William, for example.

WILLIAM WAS CONVINCED HE WAS FAILING

It was the week before finals. We'd just covered the hardest chapter of the semester, and the class had jumped to a whole new level of difficulty. As anticipated, everyone was struggling. William, who'd failed the class previously, came to see me during office hours and asked if it was possible for him to pass the class. He was convinced he wasn't going to pass but wanted to ask first before just giving up and not taking the final exam. Let me reiterate this: William thought he was failing so much that he was considering skipping the final and admitting defeat.

I did the calculations for him. The final exam was only 20 percent of his grade, and his work on everything else was so strong that he only needed to get 50 percent or higher on the final to pass the class. This was a kid who almost gave up and didn't show up to the final exam! If we hadn't done that calculation, he would've given up, when he was so close to succeeding. Even though the coursework had gotten difficult, we created a game plan to ensure he could answer over 50 percent of the questions correctly. He came to the final exam confident because he knew exactly what he needed to do to succeed.

CRUSH MATH NOW

Collect every math grade so far this semester or quarter. In your *Crush Math Now Game Plan*, write down your graded assignments and what you'll need on your remaining grades to reach your goal. Don't waste a lot of time on this. Make it quick, or ask for assistance if you can't do it quickly on your own.

OBSTACLE 2: YOUR LEVEL OF COMPETENCE

Now that you know what grade you need, let's assess the true problem: your understanding of the material. You can't improve your grade unless you improve your understanding, your skills, and your ability to answer questions correctly. This is known as your competence.

Back in the 1970s, Noel Burch, an employee with Gordon Training International, developed the "Four Stages of Competence" to help people understand the learning process better. Here's a quick overview:

1. Unconscious Incompetence: You do the wrong thing and don't understand why or what you could've done differently.
2. Conscious Incompetence: You do the incorrect thing, but you understand that it's incorrect and know what you ought to have done differently.
3. Conscious Competence: You can do the correct thing, but with much effort and concentration.
4. Unconscious Competence: You do the correct thing automatically.

Think about something you're really good at— maybe piano or soccer or talking to people. At the top of the pyramid for that skill, you know what to do and you do it automatically. You've become so good at playing piano, for instance, you do it automatically. Your fingers go to the correct place without you having to think about each movement. If your strength is playing soccer, you can dribble while scanning the field for defenders and your own teammates. You don't even need to look at the ball! If your strength is talking to people, you don't need to think about what's awkward or appropriate anymore.

You just interact naturally. Everyone has varying levels of competence at different things. Because whether it's playing Beethoven, passing the soccer ball with your left foot, or striking up a conversation with a classmate, practice makes perfect.

On the flip side, think of the first time you tried anything difficult. Like when you were a toddler and just learning to talk. Or a slightly older child learning to read. Guess what? You were really bad at it the first time you tried. You got it wrong —a lot. In fact, you didn't even know how to go about learning to read, so you followed the guidance of experts (i.e., people who could read) and deliberately practiced according to what they told you. The better their guidance and the more deliberate practice you completed, the better reader you became. It took a lot of deliberate practice to go from being an "unconsciously incompetent" reader (i.e., a child who cannot read) to a "consciously competent" reader (i.e., a child who reads automatically without sounding out words).

Whether it was obvious or not, you've spent a great deal of time honing certain skills and not others—which is perfectly fine! There isn't time to become an expert at everything. But, like it or not, to reach your goal for math, you'll need to hone some of your math skills...with deliberate practice. And to raise your grade efficiently, you don't have time to hone *all* your math skills. You must hone only the skills that impact your grade.

It's important to understand where you fall in this hierarchy in regard to your next math test. Don't get offended here. You need to be honest with yourself. If the questions on your next math test reflect the skill set you're supposed to have mastered, what is your level of competence? Here is a breakdown of how Noel Burch's levels pertain to your math test:

Level One: Unconscious Incompetence. This is when you look at your math test and you have no freaking clue. Even if you could have studied all over again, you wouldn't know what to study. You literally know so little that you are unaware of how little you know. Students never think they're unconsciously incompetent, but here's some brutal honesty: if you're failing or borderline failing, you're Unconscious Incompetent. Even if you chalk up your poor performance to slacking, there's something that you don't realize you're missing. This is the scariest level, but, thankfully, this is also the easiest level to jump out of.

Level Two: Conscious Incompetence. This is also when you look at a math test and can't solve many problems. However, unlike students who are Unconscious Incompetent, if you could have studied all over again, you'd know what to study. You recognize which skills and foundations you need to learn in order to succeed. You know what problems and skills you should've studied, and you know exactly what you should've done to learn them. This is where many passing—but struggling—students fall. If you're not here yet, don't worry: This level can be achieved with a simple diagnostic test and tracking (more on that later).

Level Three: Conscious Competence. You look at your math test and you can solve the problems, but it requires much concentration. If you're an A or B student but are struggling to reach or maintain that grade, this is where you are. You're able to do the work, but you don't know it well enough that it's second nature. While you're already where most students aspire to be, if you want a guaranteed A—or an A while putting in half the time—you need to bump yourself up to the next level.

Level Four: Unconscious Competence. You look at your math test and can solve the problems easily, as if they were "second nature." Keep in mind that this isn't a permanent state and can vary from test to test. While you may be able to solve problems on one topic automatically, you may not be able to do so in another. If you still have many more math classes down the road or simply want an expert level of understanding, you need to assess the level of your various skills. You may be at level four for integrating most Calculus problems but level three for integrating trigonometric functions. Just as with levels one to three, reaching your goal will require strengthening those weaker areas.

Most math students have varying levels of competence in specific math skills. You may be at level four for addition and multiplication (you do it naturally, automatically, without thinking about it), but level three for factoring (you can do it, but carefully, slowly, and with great effort), level two for solving complex rational equations (you know if you review factoring and simplifying rational expressions, you could get it), and level one for anything Calculus (you don't know where to start or even what foundations you'd need to learn to figure it out).

We care only about your level of competence on the math questions that will be on your next math test. You need to know which math problems you know and which you don't. Otherwise, you'll waste your time studying things you already know and not study the things you don't know.

ISABELLA, UNCONSCIOUS INCOMPETENT

It was a few weeks into the semester, and I'd sent an email out to pester my students who were behind on homework. I received a reply from a frantic student. She was so overwhelmed, she didn't know where to start. She hadn't done any homework. She hadn't even realized there *was* homework (I'm still not sure how this happened.) She couldn't even figure out how to access the online homework. She didn't know where to start to get caught up and, as her email said, she'd never been more stressed out in her life.

What Isabella didn't realize was that her freak-out was her making the important jump from Level One: Unconscious Incompetence, where she didn't realize she knew nothing, to Level Two: Conscious Incompetence, where she became conscious of the fact that she knew nothing and could now move forward with figuring out how to correct this. This was the crucial leap she needed to make to, as her email said, "work my butt off to catch up." And she did just that.

CRUSH MATH NOW

In your *Crush Math Now Game Plan*, create two lists, one titled *Know It* and the other titled *Don't Know It*. For the *Know It* list, add any questions you could answer correctly (Levels 3 and 4) if your test was today. For the *Don't Know It* list, add any skills and questions that you would answer *incorrectly* if your test was today (Levels 1 and 2). The *Don't Know It* list is the obstacle you must overcome to crush your math test.

OBSTACLE 3: YOU

The first two obstacles are the more obvious ones. Obviously, you need higher grades. Obviously, you need to understand the material better. The hard part is *how*! How do you do it? The reason why students so often cannot figure out how to solve their grades and competency problems is that they never acknowledge or solve Obstacle 3: You.

This is the hard one. This is the one that requires you to assess your personal strengths and weaknesses. This is the one that requires you to disregard anyone or anything that is to blame, except for you. Your teacher's to blame? Doesn't matter. Your parents are to blame? Video games or social media are to blame? Learning disabilities or anxiety are to blame? Totally, absolutely doesn't matter. Please note: I'm not saying these things aren't to blame. I'm saying it doesn't matter. You can't wait for these external factors to change. That's out of your control. The only solution is to overcome these external factors and succeed despite them.

"You" includes the things that *you* control, so you must focus on changing *you*. Change what you do. Change how you do things. Change when you do things. Change who you do things with. Change who you are at your core. Don't get offended by that. There isn't a written document that delineates who you are at your core. Who you are is ethereal. It's malleable. It is ever-changing and, from the day we were born, we were meant to change for the better every day of our lives. If we weren't, we'd all still be babies who couldn't walk or articulate thoughts.

So be honest with yourself. Pinpoint what obstacles you need to overcome, and then read the corresponding chapters to figure out how to overcome them.

The following are the most common and far-reaching problems I've seen students struggle with. Start with whichever one jumps out as impacting your grade the most.

Chapter 3: What to Do If You Procrastinate or Lack Motivation. You hate math and think it's pointless. You know it's a stupid requirement for your school or major, but *why* it's required is beyond you. You want hacks and shortcuts to improve your grade but couldn't care less about the math itself. If this sounds like you, your primary obstacle is a lack of motivation and you must read this chapter first.

Chapter 4: What to Do If You have Math Anxiety or Lack Confidence. You are not a math person. You're scared of math. You blank out during tests because you're nervous. You have anxiety or panic attacks during tests. You've failed math or math tests before and know, based on experience, that it's likely to happen again. Your primary obstacle ultimately boils down to math anxiety or simply not being a math person.

Chapter 5: What to Do If You Lack Grit and Discipline. You have confidence and motivation but for some reason can't bring yourself to do the work consistently. You know that if you did the work, you'd do well. You know exactly why you need to crush math; it's a goal that's important to you, but you can't bring yourself to do the work consistently. Maybe in general, you struggle to keep good habits and cut bad ones. Your primary struggle is with discipline.

Chapter 6: What to Do If You're Struggling to Succeed on Your Own. You've been trying to succeed in math all by yourself and probably for good reason. You may have a bad or unsupportive teacher. You may not have family or friends who can help you succeed. You don't have teachers or adults who are your mentors, counselors, or confidants to help you. Or perhaps you do have an awesome support system at your disposal, but you can't bring yourself to take the first step to ask them for help. Your biggest obstacle is that you are unable to succeed on your own.

Chapter 7: What to Do If You Have an Emergency or Permanent Obstacle. If you're facing an emergency, such as a medical problem, a job loss, or a parent passing, the first part of this chapter will walk you through how to deal with a temporary emergency that has wreaked havoc on your life and thrown you off course. The second part of this chapter provides strategies for crushing permanent obstacles, such as a learning disorder, English being your second language, being a parent, working full-time, or being an adult returning to school. These are problems that aren't going away anytime soon and must be dealt with while simultaneously crushing math. If your primary obstacle is overcoming an emergency or permanent obstacle, read this chapter first.

Chapter 8: What to Do If You Study Ineffectively or Just Don't Understand Math. You don't have a clear sense of what you know and don't know. You don't have a clear sense of what will be on the next test. You passively review notes and read through the book to study. You might even be making mistakes on things you should have learned last semester. You might study, but you study ineffectively and aren't actually learning what you need to know in order to ace your test. The thing that's impacting you the most is studying ineffectively and not understanding the math.

Chapter 9: What to Do If You Study and Take Tests Too Slowly. Homework takes too long. Studying for exams takes too long. You're easily distracted when doing math homework, "thinking" about homework along with the million other things bouncing around in your head. Or perhaps you are just so busy with work, parenting, or a schedule packed with classes and extracurriculars that you need to figure out how to get math done as fast as humanly possible. Your biggest obstacle is somehow related to pacing or time management.

Chapter 10: What to Do If You're Failing or Doing Poorly on Tests. You can't finish tests on time. You forget formulas and steps or make careless errors. You struggle with the longer or more complex test questions. You don't study efficiently the night before your tests. You might not even realize there are test-taking strategies for the morning of your test, the few minutes right before your test starts, or during your test. You could benefit from every hack or shortcut possible to gain points on your math exams. If your test is this week, jump right into this chapter. If you've got more time, however, tackle your other problems first and save this chapter for the week of your next math test.

HARPER, PRISCILLA, AND DYLAN'S "YOU" PROBLEMS

Looking back at Harper, Priscilla, and Dylan, each of them faced different "you" problems. If Harper were reading this book, she would have identified her problems as a bad teacher and procrastination, so she might start by reading about her flawed support system (Chapter 6) and motivation (Chapter 3). Later, she'd read about studying faster (Chapter 8) and strengthening her test-taking skills (Chapter 10), but to get to those she'd need to work through the other problems first. Without crushing excuses and tackling her motivation, none of the other strategies would have helped, because she wouldn't have bothered to implement them.

Priscilla's math anxiety was so severe, she would need to read about more than math anxiety (Chapter 4). She would also need to read about studying effectively (Chapter 8), improving her test-taking skills (Chapter 10), taking tests faster (Chapter 9), and math anxiety (Chapter 4). Even though she had a longer and more difficult journey than Harper, she'd work her way through different chapters, keep making changes, and eventually find the strategies that would help her. The lesson here is to keep experimenting. If you start off tackling the wrong problem, don't worry. Just keep at it and you will find the strategies that are right for you.

If Dylan were reading this book, he would start by reading about learning disabilities (Chapter 7). That would lead him to strengthen his foundations (Chapter 8) and sharpen his test-taking skills (Chapter 10). However, if he'd read those chapters before tackling his learning disability, he would have thought they did not pertain to him.

So, the moral of the story is: Tackle the biggest things first. Identify the problems that you *think* are impacting your grade the most, and then read those sections first. Implement those strategies first. If you think it's weird that, while working on your math grade, you're reading about the psychology of motivation, discipline, and grit—don't. The reason some math study guides can be useless is that they're not tackling the underlying issues. It's crucial to overcome your underlying issues sooner rather than later.

Think about your strengths and weaknesses. Where do you excel, and where do you need to improve? Some students have all the confidence in the world but no work ethic or game plan. Others are organized beyond belief but have no passion for the work or belief in their abilities. Whatever your strengths are, celebrate them. Whatever your weaknesses are, fix them. It's up to you to look inside yourself, acknowledge your qualities, and hone your skills. Yes, it requires introspection, but you must do it because no one else can do it for you.

CRUSH MATH NOW

In your *Crush Math Now Game Plan*, write down the two biggest problems you think are holding you back from succeeding in math. Set aside time today and tomorrow to read those chapters.

DEFINE YOUR MATH BHAG

Successful people—millionaires, professional athletes, musicians, entrepreneurs, doctors, etc.—all started their path to success with what Jim Collins and Jerry Porras, in their book *Built to Last: Successful Habits of Visionary Companies*, call "Big, Hairy, Audacious Goals," or BHAGs.

Why do your life goals need to be big, hairy, and audacious? Because only with really awesome goals and specific steps to reach those goals will you be motivated enough to work toward your goals *today*. Without clearly defined goals, you'll just waste your time playing video games, watching TV, texting for five hours straight, or staring at a wall.

If your life goals are small and measly, like, "I want to be a cashier and eventually get out of student debt," you're setting the bar too low. You'll never be motivated to succeed in math because, quite frankly, you can get by with a small, unimpressive, unexciting life without math. It's when you think big, think awesome and think monumental that you need math. So think big, think awesome, and think monumental when it comes to your life goals. After all, you only get one life. Don't get intimidated and make it small. Learn some math and make your life everything you dreamed it could be.

We're going to turn your *Obstacle 1: Your Grade* into a BHAG, but before you write out your big, hairy, audacious goal, let's look at a poorly written math goal so you can see the difference:

I want a better grade in math.

Why is this poorly written? Because it's not specific. It's generic and vague. How do you know when you've succeeded? Does a 3-percent grade increase or 10-percent grade increase count as a better grade? At what point do you get to celebrate your win? At what point do you go into emergency/survival mode to get back on track? To get more specific, answer the following questions.

What is your math BHAG? This is the grade you want on your next big test. Make it bigger, hairier, and more audacious than you think you're capable of doing. If you'd be happy with passing, aim for a B. If you really want a B, aim for an A. If you have an A, aim for a perfect A in half the study time. Make your goal big, hairy, and audacious.

What is the deadline? Mark the specific date you want to reach your goal—whether that's the date of your next exam or the end of the semester. Now, count how many days you have until that deadline. This is how many days you have to accomplish your goal. Don't worry! You can do anything for a short period of time.

Why is this your math BHAG? The longer and more detailed your WHY explanations are, the more you really want this goal, the more the goal will mean to you, and the more likely you are to see it through. Write down in detail *why* you must crush math. (Don't skip this. Come back and read your "why" statement repeatedly to keep you on track when things get tough.)

What will happen if you *don't* reach your math BHAG? Maybe it's just human nature, but many students are more motivated by negative consequences than positive ones. Write down the negative consequences that will occur—or the opportunities you'll miss out on—if you don't crush math. Maybe you won't get into the college you want. Or maybe you'll have to change majors and settle for an easier, less exciting major. Maybe you'll be embarrassed. Maybe your parents will ground you or simply be disappointed. Write down every negative consequence you can think of.

Remember, what you do today determines who you are tomorrow. If you want to be a student who has crushed math in the future, then today you must define what crushing math means to you and then create a game plan to achieve your goals.

YOUR CRUSH MATH NOW GAME PLAN

I like the term "game plan" better than "study plan." Study plans are boring, rigid, and hard to stick to. They also never work as well as you think they will. A game plan is fluid. It changes as the game goes on, with the sole purpose of winning. It assesses and adapts, never taking its eyes off the goal: winning. In your case, winning is reaching your BHAG. That's what we're creating today: a smart game plan that, as the semester passes, you'll assess and adjust as needed, always with your goal in sight. Your game plan breaks down into one single question:

What will you do to achieve your BHAG?

It's all about the work. It's all about the part that you have control over. It's all about taking responsibility for your own success. Think about what you've been doing in math up until this point, and think about the results that you're getting. If you want different results, you must change what you're doing. Make a list of all the things you need to do to accomplish your BHAG, including the things you're already doing that are working and the things that are not working (and then brainstorm possible changes).

This is the rough draft of your game plan. As you read through *Crush Math Now*, add to your game plan. Any new tactic you can try or any change you can make will strengthen your game plan. Keep changing and improving until you're getting the results you want. Your game plan is crucial to write out from day one, but by no means is it a stationary or fixed plan. It will constantly evolve, as you try different things and assess the results they give you.

Lastly, you must keep your game plan somewhere that is

easy to locate and look at. Keep it on your phone and look at it in the morning, before class, before you do homework, and even before bed just to end the day on the right mindset. Remember: out of sight, out of mind. *If you don't look at your game plan frequently, you'll forget about it.*

A GAME PLAN FOR FAILING STUDENTS

In my experience, failing students typically have trouble identifying the biggest obstacles they need they need to overcome. Therefore, instead of facing these obstacles head-on, failing students instead look for shortcuts, most of which will not help them until they've crushed the big obstacles. If you think your problem is that you're bad at taking tests, I must be honest with you: If you're failing, your problem is bigger than that. Jumping to the chapter on taking tests isn't going to help you until you fix the underlying problems.

Therefore, to give you some of the tools necessary to identify and overcome your obstacles, I recommend starting with the following chapters, in this order, if you are failing math:

1. Chapter 3: What to Do If You Procrastinate or Lack Motivation. I want you to read this chapter not because you procrastinate or lack motivation, but because you have big obstacles ahead, and you will need these strategies to combat burnout when the going gets tough.

2. Chapter 6: What to Do If You're Struggling to Succeed on Your Own. The bottom line is that you need to utilize whatever support system you have *more* than you have been. If you were properly utilizing your support system, you would not be failing. Now is not the time to worry about being a nuisance or intruding on people. Now is not the time to complain about people not being helpful. Now is the time to ask for help. In order to catch up fast enough that you will pass, you will need to take advantage of teachers, your school's tutoring center, and any other support you can access. It takes a village, and you cannot go from failing to passing without one.

3. Chapter 8: What to Do If You Study Ineffectively or Just Don't Understand Math. Whatever you are doing is not resulting in a passing grade, so you must overhaul how you study math. Try every single strategy here at least once. If you're failing, *every* change is worth trying out.

Whatever your obstacles, this should be your starting point, and you must take it seriously. You need tools to keep you motivated. You need an exact list of what you need to learn. You need a support system to expedite learning what's on the list. So read through these three chapters first and focus on changes. If, at the end of those chapters, you're not willing to try the strategies within them, then understand that failing math will not change.

And here's the truth: It's not just failing math that won't change. Some people will never be rich. They will never be happy. They will never be beautiful or healthy or find love or feel the overwhelming pride of conquering something worth conquering, mastering something worth mastering, or accomplishing something worth accomplishing. Why? Because they'll never try.

If they did try, on a whim, it would be half-assed and doomed for failure. They wouldn't put their heart into it, and they'd give up immediately. Some people are just like that. And guess what? If that's you, I don't have a pep talk for you. If you're not willing to try, you're gonna fail. If you won't take responsibility for your own success, you won't succeed. If this is you, my recommendation is to close the book because it's a waste of your time. If, at some point in the future, you're willing to try new things and make changes in your life, read the book then. Try it then.

CRUSH MATH NOW

Don't worry about three weeks from now. That's for Future You to deal with. All you can control is now. Right now, take a few minutes, do the exercises from this chapter, and write down every single thing you will do to achieve your goal. This is your *Crush Math Now Game Plan*.

3. WHAT TO DO IF YOU PROCRASTINATE OR LACK MOTIVATION

You know that you should do your homework, but you don't do it. You know you should study for that test ahead of time, but you don't. You know you should ask your teacher questions, but you don't. The problem isn't that you can't figure out math or that you aren't a "math person." The problem is that you don't have the motivation to do what you need to do.

If you don't think motivation can really be a problem, let me tell you about a student named Jared, who worked as a valet. His mom was making him go to community college. She called me and asked me to tutor Jared the night before his Statistics final exam. I will tell you right now, this kid was not motivated. He never did his homework (it was optional), he'd never gone to class (also optional), and he was hoping to pass on pure luck. As the wise Stats tutor that I was, I left him with a list of exactly what he needed to review for the remainder of the night. All he had to do was cram for one night and, because his final was worth so much of his grade, he had a shot at passing. Do you think he did the work after I left? Do you think he passed? Heck no! After I left, he didn't look at his book once. He *kinda* wanted to pass, but not enough to do his homework. Not enough to show up to class. Not even enough to study the night before his final exam. Of course, he failed.

Here's the thing: Two years later, I got another call from Jared. Not his mom this time, but Jared himself. He was still working as a valet and wanted to schedule tutoring sessions with me for Statistics. This time, we started in the first week of class, and he intended to study at both the math center and with me every week of the semester. On top of that, he was paying for school and our $100/hour tutoring himself. *Why?* Because there was no way he was going to work one more year as a valet. He was sick of it, and school was his way out. The same kid who couldn't bring himself to study the night before his final now had motivation. He passed Stats this time, and the only thing that changed was his motivation.

If you lack motivation, nothing else in this book will help you. No parent or teacher or tutor can help you. No tip or hack or study strategy can help you. So it's best to fix the motivation right from the start. Typically, students blame their lack of motivation on one of the following:

1. You believe that math is stupid and pointless.
2. You have too many goals, and math is the least important.
3. You're living in a world that hates math.
4. You're just too tired to care.
5. Everybody around you also hates math, and their hatred is contagious.

The next sections dig into each of these problems one at a time. I promise there's no math in this chapter. Although this chapter will indirectly help you in math, it's mostly about psychology.

PROBLEM 1: YOU BELIEVE THAT MATH IS STUPID AND POINTLESS.

Whatever you're spending time on, you should know *why* you're doing it. Why does one play soccer? Because it makes you healthy, it's great exercise, it's fun, it helps you make new friends, it teaches teamwork, and it affects your brain chemistry in a way that makes you happier. See how thorough the list of reasons to play soccer is? It's essential to know *why* you're playing soccer, because if you thought it was stupid and pointless, you'd never bother to show up to practice, practice on your own, or practice when you're too tired or would rather watch TV or do anything less strenuous.

The same thing goes for math. You must have strong, concrete reasons *why* you must succeed in math. Understanding *why* will provide the motivation necessary to succeed. It'll motivate you to get the work done when you don't want to do it. It'll motivate you to make sacrifices when you'd rather not, to struggle when you'd prefer the easy route, and to persevere when you want to give up. How could you possibly remain motivated enough to do math if you think it's stupid and pointless?

The problem with math is that nobody understands *why* they're learning math. When I asked my class why you need math, I got silence. Like a petulant child, I stood there and waited for somebody to give me an answer. More silence. Then, finally, a hesitant hand was raised, and a student asked, "So I know how to tip my waiter?" It made me want to cry.

So I'm not even going to ask you to write down *why* math is important because, if you're anything like my students, you will come up with inane and offensive reasons, like tipping your waiter or doing your taxes. Instead, I'm just going to tell you *why* you need math. Listen closely, because this stuff will make you rich.

Math Will Make You Less of an Idiot. People are idiots. We make idiotic decisions every day based on impulses, feelings, and a general indescribable sense of, "I want that." Don't get me wrong, I love people. We are kind, creative, funny, sympathetic, and loving, but, at the heart of all our goodness, we are still idiots. "Idiot You" wants to buy that car you can't afford, longs to kick back and watch some more TV, and thinks the world's problems are too big to solve. Idiot You is powerful. It's driven by emotion, influenced by millions of tiny things every day, and has the ultimate say in what we choose to do and not do. If you ever look at your life and think, "This is not who I wanted to be! This is not the life I imagined for myself!"—Idiot You is to blame. How do you fight back against Idiot You? Math! How do you make choices that are not idiotic? Math! What is the one thing that will save you from a life of idiocy? Math! Math will make you less of an idiot, which leads us to...

Math is the Foundation for Awesome Decision-Making. Who is going to take out a loan to buy a car when they're already drowning in student and credit card debt? Idiot You. The part of us that is not making awesome, math-based decisions. It's saying, *the car is so pretty, and I can show it off to my friends, and it'll make me happy, and the car loan guy said I can afford it, and everyone else has a newer car than me! Please, pretty please!* No. You must be able to do the math, which means you must be able to understand your credit card debt, your student loans, your car loan, your income in terms of money and health benefits and taxes and insurance, and your income in terms of hours worked. You must also think about your long-term financial goals and whether or not this car loan is in line with your long-term goals. If you follow Idiot You, you'll make an impulsive decision without understanding the consequences. If you make a math-based decision, you won't regret it, regardless of what you choose. Which leads us to...

Math Will Make You Rich. Rich people don't have student debt. They figured out how to pay it off immediately or graduate without it. Rich people don't worry about paying their bills each month because they have money saved for a rainy day. Rich people live longer. They have better healthcare. They have money that is making them more money (a.k.a. dividends, which people who know math *love*.) Being rich is awesome, and the vast majority of people who are rich—and have the wherewithal to remain rich—know math. Math has made them super awesome decision makers. Math has increased their wages and decreased their odds of unemployment. Math made them more employable, marketable, and valuable in whatever their career was. Math allowed them to stay out of or quickly minimize their debt. It allowed them to assess risk and take on debt that was smart. It helped them find and build assets, such as stocks, bonds, and real estate. No matter how much you hate math, just remember: Math will make you rich.

Math Will Teach You to Overcome Challenges. Did everything in that last paragraph sound overwhelming? Stocks, bonds, risk analysis? Yeah, that stuff gets complicated really fast, but guess what? Math teaches you to conquer hard things. Of course, math is hard. If you've had an easy life, it might even be the most difficult thing you've ever faced. If you want to be rich or successful in life, you must become the type of person who does difficult things! Embrace the challenges! Nothing worth doing is easy. Problem-solving is the greatest skill you can learn from math. Math is tedious. It requires motivation and discipline. It requires grit, problem-solving, and creativity. It requires becoming the kind of person who will succeed when life gets tough. Isn't that the kind of person you want to become? Learn to succeed in math, and you'll become the kind of person who can succeed in anything.

Math Will Help You Stay Fit. How many calories are in a Starbucks Frappuccino, how many times per week do you drink one, and how many pounds will that equate to over the next five years...said nobody ever! However, people who crush math do these simple estimations and mental math automatically. In five years, who do you think is more fit: the person who drinks 400-calorie Frappuccinos five days a week or the one who automatically does some mental math, realizes that equates to just under 150 pounds gained in five years and stops their bad habits? Math will help you get fit and healthy. Then, it will help you stay fit and healthy. If you look deeply enough, math is the foundation for everything related to health, fitness, and weight loss.

Math Will Make You Happy. Not fake Instagram happy, but genuinely, truly happy. Happy to the point that you can look back on your life and say, "If I had to do it again, I would do it exactly the same way." Conquering math will make you a stronger, prouder, smarter, and more capable person, which will lead to you being happy. Do not confuse happiness with being entertained. Don't set out to be entertained, get confused, and think that will make you happy. Eleanor Roosevelt once said, "Happiness is a byproduct of a life well-lived." So, you don't strive for happiness. You strive for a life well-lived, and happiness will find you. Part of a life well-lived is being able to look back and say, "I didn't let a little math stand in the way of my dreams." If Eleanor Roosevelt were alive today, I'm certain she would tell you that math will make you happy.

Math Will Help You Change the World. Anyone can come up with a hypothetical solution to the world's problems. Math, however, empowers you to set your solutions into motion. Here's an example. I believe that math empowers students to solve their problems and go on to live bigger, bolder lives. This is why I teach math and with some simple algebra I can see that if I teach four classes of 40 students a year for the next twenty years, then I've helped 3,200 students. Not bad. It's a small change, but it's a change nonetheless. But what if I wanted to make a bigger impact? The mathematician in me did some basic math and found that writing this book could, potentially, have a bigger impact. If I could write a book that empowers students to crush math and go on to live bigger, bolder lives, then I could potentially have a larger impact than I could with teaching alone. If this book can help 100 students and they each pass it on to 5 more students, then I've actually helped 500 students. If each of those 500 students passes it along to five more students, then I've helped 2,500 students, then 12,500, then 62,500, and so on. Math is the reason I wrote this book and, if this book able to make any impact on the world, math will be the reason I was able to do it. Math will turn you from powerless and filled with hypothetical solutions to taking concrete steps to impact the world.

Whatever your problem is, math is the answer. Sure, math is the reason I wrote this book, but math also gave me the courage and the freedom to write it. Math helped me figure out a schedule where I could make time to write. It helped me develop the grit and discipline to write every day, when there were so many easier things to do. Math is at the foundation of every awesome decision I've ever made, and I believe it can impact you in the same way.

Math will elevate your whole life. *If you look deeply enough, math is in everything.* There is math in health, in happiness, in time management, in wealth building, in career building, in friendships, in priorities, in raising kids, in getting through school. If you approach every problem you ever encounter in life with a mathematical mindset, *you will solve it*. That is the beauty of math. Used correctly, it will elevate your whole life.

To succeed in math, you must have significant, far-reaching reasons that are vital to your very being. You must truly understand, deep in your heart, *why* crushing math is essential to your goals and your life. If you don't, you'll give up as soon as it gets tough.

CRUSH MATH NOW

Set your timer for five minutes. In your *Crush Math Now Game Plan*, write down every possible reason *why* you must crush math.

PROBLEM 2: YOU DON'T MAKE SACRIFICES.

Next, take five minutes to write down every single one of your goals. Yes, first on your list is, "I want an A in math," but what about your other goals? Whether you have five or fifty more goals, write them down. Academic goals, extracurricular goals, travel goals, relationship goals, financial goals, work goals. It can be as big as "be a millionaire" and as small as "show up on time to class tomorrow." It can be a repeated goal, like "check my phone less than fifty times a day" or a one-time goal, like "go rock climbing." Whatever your goals are, you need a complete list. Write it now.

Done? Alright, why the list? Because nothing comes without sacrifice. Remember how I said that when I was touring colleges, half the seniors I asked told me they wished they'd studied more? They had sacrificed studying and academic accomplishment to have fun. The other seniors said they wish they'd had more fun. Well, they had sacrificed fun in exchange for studying and academic accomplishments. To find that perfect balance, you must be very cognizant of what you choose to do with your time. There are only so many hours in each day, so when you choose to put time toward one goal, you must acknowledge that you're sacrificing time for other things. There are always sacrifices to be made, so you might as well think about them and make conscious decisions about what you do and do not want to sacrifice.

Look at all your goals. You have your goal of crushing math. Now, pick two other goals that you *must* accomplish, two other goals that are equally as important to your future and long-term goals. Now you have three goals. These are your goals, and you will focus exclusively on them until you are finished with them. Write them down and hang them somewhere where you will see them multiple times a day. Done.

What about all your other goals? Reality check: These are not your other goals. These are your obstacles. They are actively trying to distract and sidetrack you from your goals. Do them if you must, but don't fall into the nonsensical "I can balance everything" mindset. If you're balancing all those other things but not achieving your top three goals, then your life is not in balance. The obstacles are winning. Therefore, the rest of your goals are no longer side projects or sub-goals. They are no longer things you're going to "balance" while working on your top three goals. They are the things that will spread you too thin. The things that will prevent you from putting in the time necessary to crush math and accomplish your other two most important goals. Avoid them at all costs. This doesn't mean they can't be your goal at another time, but you must crush math first. Once you're crushing math and everything you do goes on autopilot, you can pick another goal. But first, become the type of person who sticks to a goal and finishes it.

Use Obstacles as Motivation. When I was getting my Master's in Math, passing my math classes was my top priority.

Soccer, however, was what I did for fun and exercise. I didn't try to balance both of them. I knew that math came first and that soccer, which easily tempted me to stop studying, was the obstacle. Therefore, I decided that if I wanted to play soccer, math had to be done first. One semester, my homework for three math classes was due on Friday each week, and my soccer games were always on Thursday nights. If all my math was done for the week, I got to play soccer. If it wasn't, I stayed home and studied. I acknowledged that soccer was an obstacle and used it to motivate me to get my work done. You can use obstacles on your list that are fun, that you really want to do, as motivation to reach your goals. If you get all your math work done, you get to play soccer or go to that concert or take that sushi-making class. Obstacles don't have to be ignored, but they must be acknowledged. When appropriate, use them as a reward system.

PROBLEM 3: YOU'RE TOO TIRED TO CARE.

If you're just too tired to care, you must deal with your energy problem. I had chronic fatigue syndrome in high school, and I'll tell you that it's hard to get motivated when you don't have enough energy to stay awake. As someone who has always had to work hard to maintain a normal level of energy, here are some tips I've picked up over the years for waking up your brain so you're ready to solve problems and tackle challenges.

Eat for Energy. Some foods give you energy. Others suck the energy right out of you. The problem with math is that it requires intense concentration. After all, you're solving complicated problems! Therefore, before you study math, eat a snack to give you some energy. Not an energy drink or bowl of M&M's. Like a car, your body needs the proper fuel, and a car won't drive far or fast if you feed it a bowl of M&M's. Instead, try one of the following snacks: a bowl of nuts, a granola bar, a hardboiled egg, veggies and hummus, or any other food that will give you the stamina to get through a math study session without making you crash.

Exercise. You don't warm up for a marathon by running a marathon, so don't run a marathon now either. Don't exhaust yourself. Don't pull a muscle or be too exhausted or in pain to do math. Do just enough exercise to get your blood flowing, which gets your brain thinking. Do thirty jump squats or jumping jacks. Or a minute of plank. Choose something you love that will get your blood flowing right before you study math. It will help you work through problems faster and save you time in the end.

Drink a Glass of Water. As my college roommate once told me, "It takes a special kind of stupid to forget to drink water," but there are those of us who do. I love coffee so much, I can drink it 24/7, but at a certain point—for the sake of energy—I need to switch to water. Yes, as my ever-wise roommate taught me, sometimes we think we're tired, but we're really just dehydrated. Drink a glass of water with your snack before you start your math homework.

Get in a Good Mood. Nothing is worse than trying to solve hard problems when you're stressed or pissed off! It just doesn't work. Your brain shuts down, like a frozen iPad, and refuses to work. If you find yourself stressed, ticked off, or overwhelmed, you need to fix it before you start your math homework. Make a list of things you do to destress yourself. My list includes going for a run, drinking tea while reading, and talking through a problem with a friend. Sometimes I'll do a brain dump, meaning I'll write down every single thing that's stressing me out. Sometimes just getting it out of your head is enough to relieve the stress and allow you to focus.

Get Enough Sleep. I know this goes without saying, but

for some people it can be difficult to do. Want your brain to think better, remember things better, and deal with stress better? These are all side effects of getting enough sleep. Just as one really shouldn't forget to drink water, it's also important not to forget to sleep.

PROBLEM 4: YOU DON'T ADVERTISE TO YOURSELF.

Prisha gets out of bed and brushes her teeth. Next to the mirror is a note she wrote, "A on Calculus final." She goes to her closet to get dressed and on the back of the door is a copy of a (pretend) doctoral certificate with her name on it. She had printed it up to remind herself of what she's working towards. She looks at her phone and sees the Dartmouth College emblem in the background. She eats breakfast and opens a pretty journal with "Stop doubting yourself, work hard, and make it happen" inscribed on a cover. Inside, she reviews her game plan for getting an A in Calculus, the specific steps that she'll take today to work towards her goal. She finishes up and heads to school.

Saanvi also gets out of bed. While scrolling through Instagram and getting distracted down a rabbit hole of articles and other social media apps, she brushes her teeth and gets dressed. She eats breakfast, still glued to her phone and heads to school.

Prisha and Saanvi both have the same goal, to get an A in Calculus and go on to become a doctor. Just based on their morning routines, who do you think is more likely to achieve their goal? Prisha. Why? Because she advertises her goal to herself. She takes control of the things she reads and hears every day. She makes sure that her goals, her game plan, and any important messages that she needs to remember are easily visible and frequently seen.

Saanvi, on the other hand, isn't paying attention. Have you ever heard the saying, "Out of sight, out of mind?" Saanvi's goals are out of sight, so she's more likely to forget about them and not make those tiny important steps each day. The messages that she hears are the messages the rest of the world wants her to hear.

Saanvi is more likely to lose track of her goals simply by being distracted. It's easy to get lost in a noisy world that's trying to pull your attention in different directions. It's easy to drift. It's easy to get sidetracked, meander, and not grow up into the kind of person you always assumed you'd become. On the flip side, if you can hand-select specific messages that will keep you on track and that will have a positive impact on you, you can take control back. You can grow in the right direction. You can make progress towards your goals. I've yet to come across a universal term for this, but because it parallels the way companies advertise to us, I'll call it advertising to yourself.

How do you advertise to yourself? You figure out what your goals and game plan are. You figure out what messages you need to hear every day. Do you need messages to boost your confidence? Or messages to remind you to buckle down and do the work? Find places where you'll automatically see your goals, your game plan, and your hand-selected messages. Put them in places that are easy and convenient, places you'll see them automatically without having to put in any effort.

Over the years, I've experimented a bit with this, and here's what works for me. Of all the motivational quotes out there, the one that really gets me is "Your Goals Don't Care How You Feel." It hangs in front of my treadmill and encourages me to run just a little faster or a little harder. It also hangs above my desk and encourages me to write just a little more or a little better. It reminds me to toughen up when I'm feeling lazy and it reminds me to focus when my mind starts to wander. The other thing I did is I created a file in Google Drive (though you could also use Evernote or another similar app), where I write down my goals for the year, the quarter, and the week. I skim through it most mornings while I drink coffee and it helps me assess what I need to do for the day. Often, the many "urgent" things that it feels like I need to do are not steps toward any long-term goal. This helps me prioritize a little better every day.

Successful students live in an environment that reminds them of their goals. They understand that it's not the outside world's job to motivate them, so they create a motivating environment themselves. Advertise to yourself. It's such a simple way to increase your motivation.

A QUICK NOTE ABOUT VIDEO GAMES, SOCIAL MEDIA, AND TV

If you are struggling with math, *temporarily* cut back on video games, social media, and TV until you're succeeding in math. These are three things that take up lots of time, but aren't actively moving you towards your goal of crushing math.

Do the math: If you watch one hour of television a day, that adds up to seven hours this week that you can instead put towards math. If you spend five hours a day playing video games (which some students do!), that's thirty-five hours you could put towards math in just one week. This is where you find the time to crush math quickly.

Video games, social media and TV are a multi-billion-dollar industry vying for your attention. Their goal is to get and keep your attention at all costs, and they have no financial incentive to help you put in the time necessary to crush math. It's just not part of their bottom line. Reduce your time spent on these distracting endeavors until you're crushing math.

If you're thinking that you're pretty sure you can crush

math without cutting back, then I want you to remember our talk about sacrifices. This is part of what needs to be sacrificed to crush math. Not sure you want to? Here's a question: If you fail math or fail to reach your goals because you wouldn't *temporarily* give up TV, video games, and social media, will you look back at high school or college and say, "Heck yeah! If I had to do it over again, I'd do it exactly the same!"? No! Nobody ever wishes they let obstacles as small and pitiful as TV, video games, or social media stand in their way! There are students who are struggling to work forty hours a week, keep a roof over their family's heads, and keep their babies fed, while they crush math—now, *they* have obstacles! If they can figure out how to make that happen, you can figure out how to give up a few hours of TV, video games and social media.

Even if you don't think this a problem that pertains to you, I encourage you to try the following.

Track your time. Don't start by saying, "I can balance it," or, "I don't watch five hours!" Just start by tracking your time spent watching TV, playing video games, or using social media today. Add up the time and multiply that by seven. That's how many hours per week you are losing to TV, video games and social media. Often, it's more than you realize.

Go cold turkey. If you're struggling in math, my advice is to cut TV, video games, and social media altogether until you've pulled your grades up. Get out a piece of paper and write the following note to yourself:

Dear Future Me,

Starting today, I am taking a break from *all* TV, video games, and social media until I am crushing math. You're welcome. You're more awesome because of the sacrifices I am making today.

Warmly, __[name]__

Instead of watching mindless TV, playing video games or scrolling through your phone, put in the extra time to crush math.

Upgrade the content. Are you watching and reading things that motivate you? Or are they just distractions from your goals? How is it impacting you? How do you feel afterward? Now that you have actual data of time spent, decrease the amount of time on TV, video games and social media and increase the value of the content you do watch. Listen to motivating podcasts and watch Ted Talks.

Read. What about the end of the day, when your homework and studying are all done and you're too mentally exhausted to put extra time towards pulling up your math grade? Read *Digital Minimalism* by Cal Newport, *The Little Black Book of Workout Motivation* by Michael Matthews (which will do more than motivate you to work out), or *The Miracle Morning for College Students* by Hal Elrod and Natalie Janji. If you lack motivation, read books that motivate you. Read about people who have overcome challenges, have bounced back from failure, or just inspire you.

We all get the same number of hours in a day, and the person who watches less TV, plays fewer video games, and spends less time on social media has more productive hours in the day.

PROBLEM 5: YOUR FRIENDS AND FAMILY HATE MATH.

Successful math students tend to hang out with successful math students. Mediocre math students tend to hang out with mediocre math students. Failing math students tend to hang out with—you guessed it—failing math students. If you want to change your grade, change who you study with.

If everyone around you is lazy, sleeps in, and reacts to life all day, aren't you likely to do the same thing? Won't waking up with purpose and drive and working your butt off seem weird to them? Navy Seals don't hang out with lazy couch potatoes. They hang out with other badass warriors, people who understand their drive, their purpose, and their goals. As a student who wants to succeed in math, you need to do the same.

Right now, think about the five people you spend the most time with. Write down their names. How motivated are they? What's their perspective on challenges, like math? Do they encourage you or distract you? If you're surrounded by people who hate math, think math is too hard or too pointless, or generally don't like to put in hard work and effort, then that is affecting you. You need to make an effort to surround yourself with people who can encourage and motivate you. You need to make an effort to surround yourself with people who are crushing math.

There are a couple of ways to do this. First, think of the other people you know. Are there people who are successful in math who you could study with or spend more time with? Who are the strongest math students in your class? Are they approachable? Would they help you out?

If this is an area where you need help, I encourage you to read Chapter 6 for more specific ideas to overhaul or create from scratch a kickass support system.

HOW TO MAINTAIN MOTIVATION

The crux of maintaining motivation is to turn things that would normally distract you into rewards that will motivate you. Yes, rewards work fantastically well for creating habits and meeting short-term goals. For example: If I finish assignment X, I will receive or do reward Y. If I do not finish assignment X, I will punish myself by refusing myself reward Y.

Because people respond better to punishment than rewards, don't forget the punishment.

To do this, make a list of everything you need to do today to make progress toward your top three goals and the rewards you will get if you get everything done. At the end of the day, go through it. Did you get every important thing done today that you needed to get done? If yes, then reward yourself. Watch some TV. Play a video game. Eat a dessert. Hang out with a friend. Do something you love. Do something fun. If there's something you love to do or something that relaxes you or is just plain fun, you don't have to forgo it completely just because it isn't in line with your goals. Instead of letting it be a distraction that keeps you from your goals, use it as a reward for meeting your goals or as a punishment for not meeting your goals.

This means that if you didn't get your work done, you must forgo the reward and get the work done instead. At the end of every night, if I've done my work, I watch some TV or have a glass of wine. If I haven't, I use that time to catch up on my work.

Now, that's one way to motivate yourself on a daily basis, but to accomplish your long-term goals, you'll need to build in bigger, bolder rewards at different milestones to keep you motivated. Just as you should build breaks into your life, you should also build in rewards. Here's a breakdown of rewards to build in on your way to crushing math:

Semester Rewards. If your final grade in math is an A, how will you reward yourself? What will you do to celebrate? Don't decide at the end of the semester after it happens. Decide now, look forward to it, and use it to motivate you to study harder and meet your goals. Right after finals is a great time for a trip! Plan to do something extra special for yourself, if you pass with an A...and plan *not* to do it, if you don't get an A.

Test Rewards. If your grade on your next math test is an A, how will you reward yourself? Go out with friends? Head out to dinner or a concert? Buy yourself something special? Whatever it is, make it something you can look forward to and which will be worth making sacrifices leading up to the test.

Weekly Rewards. During my Master's program, I had tons of math homework due on Fridays. As mentioned previously, I also played soccer on Thursday nights with friends who liked to play beer pong after the soccer games. If I got all my work done for the week by 7 pm on Thursday, I would let myself go play soccer and afterward grab a beer with my friends and play beer pong. If I got enough, but not all, of my work done, I would play soccer, but I wouldn't go out afterward. If I really didn't get my work done, then I had to skip both. On top of that, the team depends on players showing up, so there was extra motivation to not let my team down by not showing up.

Daily Rewards. What's your end-of-the-day reward for getting everything done? A TV show or video game? Time to talk to your friends? If you do these things before your work is done, they're distractions and you know that, so you won't enjoy them as fully. If you have these rewards after you finish your work, you get to enjoy them guilt-free.

For the rewards and punishments system to work, you really must experience it to understand the power behind it. Really psych yourself up for the punishment of not doing what you need to do. Don't just "not eat" the ice cream. Scoop it out, look at it, and then throw it in the trash. Don't just "not" put money toward the trip; take out cash and flush it down the toilet. Sit in front of the TV, with it turned off, and do your math homework, knowing you could be watching Netflix.

Once you've committed to the punishment, once you've experienced it, once you realize that you will stick to that punishment, it is far, far stronger than a reward system.

NOW THAT YOU'RE MOTIVATED

Take responsibility for your own success. Ultimately, you know that if you want to raise your math grade, you must study. You must study differently than before, better than before, faster and more purposefully than before. There is no skipping the studying part. You must prepare, prepare, prepare.

Now that you're motivated enough to study, here are the super obvious tips on raising your math grade. It's stuff you already know but may have been too unmotivated to actually do.

- Do all your homework, if it's required.
- Do all homework, even if it's not required.
- If doing homework isn't enough to earn the grade you want, do more than the homework.
- Do homework on time.
- If it's hard, do homework earlier than usual.
- Re-do or review homework questions you don't understand.
- Read your textbook to figure out homework questions you don't understand.
- Ask your friends about homework questions you don't understand.
- Ask your teacher about homework questions you don't understand.
- Take responsibility—somehow—for understanding questions you don't understand.
- Keep an ongoing list of questions you don't

understand and constantly work on figuring them out.

- Create your own practice quizzes.
- Take your own practice quizzes.
- Study questions in a test-like setting.
- Study every day.
- Study every day for longer than you did before.
- Study every day differently than you did before.
- Study with different people than you did before.
- Study the textbook.
- Study your notes.
- Study your mistakes.
- Study prerequisites you don't know.
- Study hard questions.
- Study at the upper edge of your abilities.
- Study anything that's not on this list but which you know ought to be studied.
- Take responsibility for your success and prepare, prepare, prepare.

CRUSH MATH NOW

Go back to Chapter 2 and create a game plan to crush math. Make sure you expand on *why* you must crush math. Then, pick the one strategy from this chapter that will have the biggest impact on your grade. Do it now, even if it's inconvenient.

4. WHAT TO DO IF YOU HAVE MATH ANXIETY OR LACK CONFIDENCE

You're just not a math person. You're bad at it. Some people get it easily, and you don't. Maybe you're afraid of math, too. Afraid to make mistakes, afraid to try, afraid of being embarrassed in class, afraid of wasting your time, energy, and effort, just to verify that you're bad at math. The fear stresses you out and follows you everywhere. You get tense and nervous during math tests. You freeze up or blank out. You can't remember formulas. You can't think straight, and you make stupid mistakes on problems you know how to solve. It's not just a confidence issue, though. Your fears are justified because you're not getting the grades you want in math. Every test you take (and do poorly on) validates the fact that you're "not a math person."

In addition to the anxiety that arises from "not being a math person," lack of confidence can have a huge impact on both your grades and your work ethic. It encourages you to work less on math (because what's the point of putting in more time, if you still won't get it?). It encourages you to give up easily (because what's the point of trying, if you still won't get it?). It encourages you to procrastinate (because what's the point of even starting, if you still won't get it?). It encourages you to freak out on tests (because you obviously can't do math, regardless of how much you prepare). It encourages you to believe that you can't understand the math before you even try. Not being a "math person" seriously sucks.

Rest assured, there are things you can do to overcome your lack of confidence. For the purpose of this chapter, I assume you are a worst-case scenario. You have math PTSD, meaning you've failed math in the past, and it's traumatized you. Much like Priscilla in Chapter 1, you have full-fledged panic attacks during tests. Your fears are legitimate because you've failed math before (perhaps several times). If you go into your next test with the low confidence you have today, you will fail it. Even if you don't have worst-case scenario confidence, this chapter will still help you. You're already a step or two in the right direction; good job! So, let's turn you into a "math person." And, since you're not a "math person," you'll be happy to know that you don't need math to accomplish this! This change is rooted in psychology. I don't know about you, but I think psychology is fascinating.

PSYCHOLOGY 101

First, let's define three important psychology terms. A student's *mindset* is their set of attitudes and beliefs. Students with a *fixed mindset* believe their intelligence and talents are fixed traits. Students with a *growth mindset* believe that their intelligence and talents can be developed through dedication and hard work.

These mindset terms are important for several reasons. First, students rarely analyze where their attitudes and beliefs come from or the impact that these beliefs have on their lives.

Second, whether you have a fixed mindset or a growth mindset has an enormous impact on your success in math. As Jo Boaler, my math professor hero and author of *Mathematical Mindsets: Unleashing Students' Potential through Creative Math, Inspiring Messages and Innovative Teaching*, states, "A lot of scientific evidence suggests that the difference between those who succeed and those who don't is not the brains they were born with, but their approach to life, the messages they receive about their potential, and the opportunities they have to learn."

Did you get that? "*The difference between those who succeed and those who don't is not the brains they were born with, but their approach to life.*" I cannot stress to you how important this is, so I'm going to say it a third time. Your success does not depend on the brain you were born with. Your success depends on your approach to life, on whether you believe that your intelligence and talents can be developed through dedication and hard work. Got it?

How does this relate to math? It doesn't. Not yet, anyway. Math is a whole other ballgame, but it does relate to most everything that you've ever considered yourself good or bad at. Let me explain with a personal experience.

ALLISON, THE SOCCER PLAYER

I am not a "natural" athlete. My parents signed me up for soccer when I was a kid, and the truth is that, no, I was not a "natural." Some kids naturally chased the ball, were fast and aggressive, and walked onto the field the first day understanding dribbling. When I first walked onto the field, even running didn't come naturally. Once I got better at running, I couldn't focus on the game. I chased butterflies and didn't know where the ball was. I talked to friends instead of knowing where the ball was. I zoned out and stared into space...instead of knowing where the ball was. For years, I had no idea how to kick, dribble or sense where on the field the ball might go next. What did my parents do? They *tricked me*, using psychology, and by the time I entered junior high and high school, I considered myself not just a soccer player, but a true, bonafide athlete. How did they do it? They helped me develop a growth mindset, and they did this through the following:

- They taught me the foundations I needed (like learning to run, kick, etc.).
- They praised my effort to learn and my hard work, rather than my actual abilities.
- When my skills lacked, they pointed out that it was something I hadn't practiced enough. It was a matter of putting in the work.
- They taught me that my mistakes were lessons to learn from and ways to grow.

They taught me *why* soccer was important. After all, I didn't want to grow up to be one of those lazy couch potatoes who go through life without the joy and health benefits of sports!

There were no special coaches or soccer hacks. There also weren't obsessive 24/7 soccer drills. They used good, old psychology-based mind tricks on me. I played on all-star teams, my high school JV team, and in co-ed soccer leagues throughout my twenties. Today, I coach my kids' soccer teams. I never became good enough to play college soccer or get a scholarship, but I became enough of a soccer player that it's brought decades of benefits to my life.

LEARNING ANYTHING DIFFICULT REQUIRES A GROWTH MINDSET

This includes learning any sport. Or any language. Or any instrument. Or any skill that develops over time and requires practice, grit, and the belief that you can do it.

Think about the things you're good at. You can probably acknowledge, at least to yourself, that it took practice and hard work to get you to where you are. Whether you vocalized it or not, you learned from your mistakes, made improvements through hard work, and persevered through the difficulties. The more praise you got, the harder you worked, the more you believed in yourself, and the more quickly you improved. Then, somewhere along the line, you became "naturally" good at something.

The same goes for math. (Yes, this all comes back to crushing math!) Math is a skill, just like a sport or a language or an instrument, that is difficult enough to require practice, grit, and the belief that you can do it. It is a skill that requires you to learn from your mistakes, make improvements through hard work, and persevere through the difficulties. Most importantly, it requires a growth mindset, because, without a growth mindset, you'll never buckle down, practice enough to improve and endure when the going gets tough. You must crush this nonsensical notion that you're "not a math person." There is no such thing as "not a math person." There are simply people who have practiced more, those who have learned from their mistakes more, and who have endured more.

Just as my parents' goal was not to turn me into a professional soccer player, our goal isn't to turn you into a Nobel Prize-winning mathematician, or even a math major. Just as my parents wanted me to get good enough at soccer that I reaped the benefits of enjoying a sport, our goal is to get you good enough at math that you reap the benefits of crushing math.

Whether it's increasing your problem-solving skills or opening doors to dream colleges, majors, or jobs, crushing math will bring lifelong benefits.

Think of math as the mental version of soccer. Soccer makes you more fit, stronger, and healthier physically. Math makes you more fit, stronger, and healthier mentally.

But what if you don't have someone in your life who has helped you develop a growth mindset? How do you trick your fixed mindset brain into embracing a growth mindset? You're in luck. I've got some ideas, but first let's look closer at the pivotal moment that transformed both Harper's and Priscilla's confidence.

THE FIRST BIG WIN

The thing that will boost your confidence the most will be your first big win. The first quiz or test you do well on. After all, you're not a fool. You know your own history. You know what you've been capable of so far, and you can't throw that all out the window and blindly believe, "You can do it!" There's no depth to those words. They're meaningless. At first, you'll have to go through the motions with these strategies, take a leap of faith that they *might* work, and know that the one thing that makes sense is coming soon. Once you succeed, you'll be able to believe that you're capable of succeeding. Once you succeed, you'll gain confidence.

Let's look at Harper's and Priscilla's first big wins. Harper was failing and had no confidence, but it was the first time she had ever severely fallen behind in math. Every time we met, I encouraged Harper to try. I told her "You can do it!" or "Just keep trying!" or "Believe in yourself!" and hoped that my enthusiasm and encouragement would sink it. She didn't believe any of it, but she went through the motions. When did her confidence actually increase? The moment she got her first A. What's the moral of Harper's story? Do the confidence building exercises, even if you're not buying into it. You won't see their impact until your first big win and there's a lag time between when you start and when you get that win. When you eventually have that win, your confidence will skyrocket. Wait for it. Do the work and it will come.

Priscilla had a much deeper-rooted lack of confidence than Harper did, but she went through the same process as Harper. She had been trying hard for years, but kept failing. Her family, friends, and teachers had encouraged her for years, but she was still failing. Hearing positive affirmations like "You can do it!" or "Just keep trying!" or "Believe in yourself!" fell on deaf ears because she'd tried hard for years and was still failing. Even when Priscilla succeeded on her practice tests, she didn't believe any words of encouragement. She didn't believe a single word of it until...she got her first passing grade. Only after her first passing grade did she believe that she was capable of passing.

Every single one of my students who has jumped from "not being a math person" to "totally being a math person" can identify the exact test or quiz grade that changed them. They will always remember that first big win. In fact, email me at allison@crushmathnow.com when you reach that win. This moment is transformational and will impact how you approach challenges for the rest of your life.

Keep this in mind as you read through the following examples. Much of what you'll find in this chapter will help give you enough confidence *to try*. To *try* to do the work. To *try* new strategies. To *try* to remember things on exams. To think maybe it's possible if I *try*. It'll lay the groundwork of building your confidence and show you tips to prepare in a way that will keep your anxiety in check. Ultimately, though, your confidence won't make leaps until you've had that first success. So for right now, I need a little trust from you. Go through the motions. Make changes to have a more positive outlook, to develop a growth mindset, to better prepare for the exam. Make changes to counter your anxiety during your next exam. Then, when you have your first big win, your first successful test, your first experience crushing math, it won't be a leap of faith anymore. You'll see proof that it's working, and your confidence will increase. Once your confidence is up, everything else will fall into place.

There's some groundwork you must lay before your first win. Without this groundwork, you could have a "first big win" that doesn't change your confidence. Without this groundwork, you'll chalk the win up to luck and keep on believing, despite evidence to the contrary, that you're not a math person.

Now, for the groundwork, there are several primary reasons why students lack confidence in math:

1. Lack of Preparation
2. Fixed Mindset Messages
3. Fear of Failure
4. Unfounded Fears

Let's take a look at each.

CAUSE 1: LACK OF PREPARATION

I'll be honest here. No matter how much you've studied, a lack of confidence in part stems from a lack of preparation. The more inadequately prepared students are, the more they lack confidence. And time spent studying counts for nothing here. The only thing that matters is whether you studied efficiently enough to learn the material. So, if you lack confidence, you need to dissect where you're inadequately prepared. Use the following exercises to figure this out.

Step 1: Ask Yourself, "What Questions Am I Afraid Of?" This is the crucial question that must be asked. Be honest with yourself. Go through what will be on the next test. What topics or questions are you afraid will be on the test? Don't just browse through your notes and think about it. Make a list of specific questions from homework, notes, quizzes, and the textbook. A list for a Chapter 3 test might look like this:

- Textbook: 3.2, page 134, examples #5 & 6
- Notes: Wednesday, 3.2, last example
- Notes: Friday, 3.4, word problem
- Homework: 3.2, #24-26
- Homework: 3.3, #29
- Homework: 3.4, all word problems!

In your *Crush Math Now Game Plan*, write down the problems you're afraid you'll see on the test. You've just taken the vague, scary, seemingly insurmountable challenge of studying for your test and turned it into a specific to-do list. For most students, the best way to crush math anxiety is to be prepared.

Step 2: Brain Dump. I use this whenever I get stressed out myself, and, as a tutor, I've used the "brain dump" method with several students as well. Simply write down a list of everything that's stressing you out about math. Then, brainstorm three solutions for each item on the list. Is homework taking too long? Is homework not getting done? Are you panicking about your test? Or panicking about particular problems on the test? Or panicking about making careless errors or running out of time or forgetting formulas on the test? The more specific you can get, the more specific your solutions will get.

Step 3: Rephrase Problems or Negative Beliefs as Questions. I covered this in the Introduction, but it's worth revisiting in the context of math anxiety. Rephrase each problem or negative belief you have as a question. For example, rephrase thoughts such as, "I am going to fail again," to, "What changes can I make so that I don't fail again?" If you are thinking, "I am going to blank out and forget everything," rephrase this as, "What can I do differently so that I don't blank out?" Focus on change. *Every problem is just a question with a solution that needs to be found.* Solutions are typically found by changing what you're doing.

Step 4: Separate Realistic and Unfounded Fears. Some fears are realistic. *If you haven't done any homework, your problem isn't dealing with anxiety.* It's needing to prepare. In that case, go read Chapter 8 to learn how to crush how you currently study and replace it with something that works. If your lack of confidence comes from lack of preparation, skip the rest of the chapter and go prepare.

If, however, you are overly prepared—you've done all the homework, gone to office hours, studied a ton, and know the material inside out—then you're facing unfounded fears. If this is you, read the rest of this chapter.

CAUSE 2: FIXED MINDSET MESSAGES

Let's dig a little deeper into what influences your mindset here. To explain further, let's take a brief detour to commercials. The average American watches five hours of TV per day, and roughly one-quarter of every hour is advertisements. That adds up to over 450 hours (or 19 days) of watching advertisements each year. And why do companies shell out over $151 billion dollars each year on advertising? Not to enlighten you. Not to educate you. Not out of the goodness of their hearts. It's because they know that what you see and hear consistently will gradually influence your thinking.

So, over the course of your lifetime, you've been getting over an hour each day of advertisers telling you that buying their products will make you happy! Your brain, much like the brains of many Americans, is likely on a broken loop of thinking: *If I buy that, I'll be happy...* When, in fact, it's crushing math that will make you happy. If car companies shelled out as much money to advertise math as they did cars, you'd believe me.

So, given the power that fixed mindset messages can have on a student, I want you to think about the thoughts and conversations that are often being repeated in your head. How many times have you heard your parents, friends, or even teachers say: *You're just not good at math. You're just not a math person. You don't do well on math tests. Math is just too hard. Math is just something you struggle with.* Now, those are just the messages you've heard from others. In addition to that, what messages do you say to yourself? It's quite possible that your brain is on a broken loop of thoughts, like *I suck at math. I can't do it. I'm terrible at math. I can't do it.* And, unfortunately, the truth is, if you think you can't, you probably can't.

So, how do you change your mindset? How do you fix your brain so you start to believe that you can crush math? You take control of the messages you read and hear every day. Just like advertisers try to inundate you with advertisements of their products, you must try to inundate yourself with growth mindset messages. How do you do that?

Surround Yourself with People Who Have a Growth Mindset. First, start spending time with people who have a growth mindset. Write down the names of the people you spend the most time with. Then, write down what their perspectives are on math. Do they have a fixed mindset, meaning they think you are just naturally bad at math? Or do they have a growth mindset, meaning they approach math and life with the idea that if anyone tries and works hard, they'll succeed?

Spend more time with the people on your list who have a growth mindset. Make those your go-to people, as you make this journey from struggling with math to crushing it. If your list includes friends and family, who have a fixed mindset, be aware of this. If someone has a negative impact on you, cut back your time spent with them, be aware of how the things they say affect you and don't let their perceptions of you define you. You are a hard-working and capable student. You are changing how you think about math and how you view yourself. You are changing from struggling with math and feeling powerless to crushing math and being in control. Don't let your mom, dad, teacher, or friend bring you down and doubt yourself.

Now, what if everyone on your list has a fixed mindset? Then, you've pinpointed precisely where your lack of confidence in math comes from, and you have a clear path forward. Seek out people with a growth mindset. Make a new list of teachers, family members, friends, and classmates who have a growth mindset, who will encourage you, who believe that hard work is more important than natural ability. Seek these people out. Study with them. Go to them for advice and encouragement. Make them a part of your life and, simply by spending more time with them, you will gradually learn to embrace this powerful new mindset.

Find Your Professor Towse. One of the reasons I majored in math, eventually went on to become a math professor, and am now writing this book is because of one professor, Professor Chris Towse, at one tiny liberal arts college, Scripps College. Why? Because he epitomized growth mindset and taught me what all the professors at Scripps teach: to love math and to love challenges. He taught me to love the hard work and the struggle. He taught me to endure when the going got tough and when I felt overwhelmed. He taught me to focus on the journey rather than just the end result.

I know that not every math department is like Scripps', but I know that hidden within every math department is at least one Professor Towse. Even if most of your math department seems stuffy and discouraging, I challenge you to find your Professor Towse. Find the professor or teacher who will encourage you and help you develop into the kind of person who can crush math. Find that one awesome role model and you'll be amazed at how much one person can positively impact your life. Find your Professor Towse.

While it might seem strange to improve your math grade by analyzing and changing the people you go to for help, it's effective. I'll give you a few more strategies for developing a growth mindset below, but if you're surrounding yourself with only fixed-mindset friends, family, and teachers, the remaining strategies might not be enough.

Binge Read Books that Embody Growth Mindset. You have so much assigned reading already that the last thing you may want to do is read books on your own, but *books that you choose* can be powerful. I didn't understand this until college when, in the library, I stumbled across *How to Win Friends and Influence People* by Dale Carnegie. I was looking for another book and the title caught my attention. I was a freshman struggling to make new friends, so I started reading. Five hours later, in the aisle in the library, I was still reading and I had this realization: Sometimes, the most helpful books, the books that teach you the stuff you actually need in real life, are not always the books that are assigned in school.

If the main thing holding you back is a fixed mindset, then an effective strategy is to read books about growth mindset or books that embody a growth mindset. Books like *Mathematical Mindsets* by Jo Boaler or *Grit* by Angela Duckworth can teach you about mindset in greater depth. The more you understand growth mindset, the easier it is to embrace it. On the other hand, books like *Vision to Reality* by Honoree Corder (my favorite), *The Miracle Equation* by Hal Elrod (my other favorite) or *Discipline Equals Freedom* by Jocko Willink (my husband's favorite) are powerful in a different way. While they don't academically dissect growth mindset, they certainly embody it. It's as if the authors themselves become your friends and the words on the page are the things your growth-mindset friends would tell you. When you have a shortage of positive, encouraging friends, binge read positive encouraging books.

Advertise Growth Mindset Messages to Yourself. The next most effective strategy for developing a growth mindset is to literally advertise it to yourself. How? Think about how advertisers advertise to you. Where do they find you? Everywhere. On the TV. On the computer. On your phone. On the radio. On billboards. In the mail. Everywhere they can possibly get their message in front of you, they do. You need to advertise growth mindset messages to yourself with the same intensity. Take your goals and favorite growth mindset quotes, for example. Where would you put them? When should you look at them?

You don't need a lot of messages, just a few that really speak to you. For example, on the wall by my treadmill is a sign that reads, "Your Goals Don't Care How You Feel." It's one message, but for me it's a powerful one. It's not advertised to me everywhere, just the one place I need it. Does it help me keep running, when I'd rather take a break and walk? Absolutely. Does it help me run longer or faster or set higher goals for myself? Absolutely.

Is there a quote that, if posted on the wall above your desk, will help you buckle down and get through your math homework? That will help you keep going when you're struggling and want to give up? Maybe "Your Goals Don't Care How You Feel" doesn't quite work, but another message might. Try out one of the following:

- *It's not that I'm so smart, it's just that I stay with problems longer.*—Albert Einstein
- *Be intrigued by mistakes, enjoy effort and keep on learning.* —Carol Dweck
- *A Calculus student is just a Prealgebra student who never gave up.*—Allison Dillard
- *It does not matter how slowly you go so long as you do not stop.*—Confucius
- *Whether you think you can or you think you can't, you're right.*—Henry Ford
- *Our greatest weakness lies in giving up. The most certain way to succeed is always to try just one more time.*— Thomas Edison
- *You must do the thing you think you cannot do.* —Eleanor Roosevelt

Keep an eye out for a message that speaks to you and place it so you'll see it when you need it most. You can put it on your closet door, so you see it when whenever you get dressed. Or next to your bathroom mirror, so you see it when whenever you brush your teeth. Or on the inside of your math book or notebook, so you see it whenever you do math. Or on your cell phone background, so you see it whenever you look at your phone. Or on the wall above your desk, so you see it whenever you sit down to study. Choose the best places for you and tape, type, or write a growth mindset message there now.

CAUSE 3: FEAR OF FAILURE

Some students are terrified of making mistakes, viewing it as proof that they're no good at math. Instead, look at your mistake, learn from it, and then...ta-da! Realize that you've just learned something. Mistakes are proof that you're tackling something difficult, that you're actually learning, that you're doing something worth doing. Failure, as it turns out, is a crucial step in the journey toward success.

Here are a few epic failures worth noting:

- Michael Jordan was cut from his high school basketball team.
- J.K. Rowling was once a jobless single mom fighting depression and living on unemployment.
- Steve Jobs was fired from Apple, the very company he founded.
- Abraham Lincoln lost elections for the state legislature, Congress (twice), the Senate (twice), and the Vice Presidency.
- Jack Canfield's *Chicken Soup for the Soul* book was rejected by 144 publishers.

Stop being afraid of failure. Recognize it as a chance to toughen up and learn something. Here are simple ways to change how you think about failure:

Understand the purpose of failure. Students who succeed in math use failure as a wake-up call. Making mistakes and not being able to solve problems are opportunities to learn. Research shows that when you make mistakes and learn from them, your brain grows. Yes! You actually get smarter when you make mistakes and learn from them. So, if you want to develop your brain, take hard math classes where you'll make lots of mistakes and learn a lot. Everybody fails at many points in math. It's how you react to failure that determines whether you'll succeed.

Embrace your imperfections. A warrior may have holes in her armor, but she goes to war anyway. You may be imperfectly prepared for your math test, with gaps of knowledge or flaws in your personality or outlook, but give it everything you've got just the same. If you're 100% perfectly prepared for your math test, then you're in a class that's not difficult enough for you. If you're imperfectly prepared, but giving it everything you've got, then you're challenging yourself and growing. You don't want to tackle things that are easy for you. You want to grow.

Settle for less than perfect. If you're 100% perfectly prepared for your math test, you're in a class that's not challenging enough for you. Some students with anxiety get too nervous to start because they want to finish 100 percent of their homework. They don't think they can get 100 percent, so why bother starting? I had one student, Camila, who would get so anxious that she wouldn't start the homework if she didn't think she could do all of it. Why start if you can't do all of it? In order to combat this, I had her aim for less than 100 percent. She would aim to do 80 percent of the homework, and then would ask for help for the last 20 percent. Usually, once she hit the 80 percent mark, she could make it through the rest. The goal was set simply to get her started. Settle for less than perfect.

CAUSE 4: UNFOUNDED FEARS

If you are thoroughly prepared but are still drowning in anxiety, I suggest the following "fear cures:"

Fear Cure 1: Take a Practice Test. Remember Priscilla,

the student who had failed Precalculus three times? We conquered her anxiety by giving her practice tests. I'd pick out random homework problems, type them up to make them look like a scary test, and have her sit down in the library and work through the problems while being timed. By doing this, she was able to *practice powering through her paralyzing fear.* As a teacher, I recommend that all of my students with anxiety do this.

Fear Cure 2: Meditate. Don't skip this! *There's actual science behind how meditation affects your brain.* It slows down certain parts of your brain, which slows down how we process information and helps us focus better. It loosens certain (bad) neural pathways (so we feel calmer), reduces our reactions (so we panic less), and increases self-awareness. It increases matter in the hippocampus, which has the side effect of more positive thoughts and increased focus. If you have math anxiety, try out the free Headspace app and, for the next five days, do a 5-minute meditation before you study math. Some of my students with math anxiety swear by this one! If you have math anxiety, try meditation.

Fear Cure 3: Make a Win List. I've gotten fed up a couple of times with students because they've claimed not to know "*Anything.*" Seriously? *Anything?* You know 2+2, right? That's *something*! So, to drive my point home, I'd write out a list of all the things they *do* know...and usually it turns out there's a lot, or at least a lot more than they think. I'm not sure which was more beneficial, me getting fed up and scolding them or the fact that they left with what I now call a "Win List," a.k.a. a list of math problems or concepts they know. Keeping a list of what you know can help build your confidence. As your Win List grows longer, your confidence will increase and your anxiety will decrease. As you add more concepts to the list, you will also study more efficiently and pinpoint areas to focus on.

Fear Cure 4: Read and Write About Your Fears. Stanford University psychologist Christopher Rozek led a study that tested the effectiveness of different methods of dealing with test anxiety before biology exams. The study found that students who were asked to acknowledge their test-taking fears, and then read and/or write about their fears, received higher test scores than the control group of students who were simply asked to ignore their fears and power through. This was a particularly effective strategy for low-income students.

Fear Cure 5: Create an Alter Ego. In his book *The Alter Ego Effect: The Power of Secret Identities to Transform Your Life*, top performance expert Todd Herman talks about creating a heroic alter ego to tap into when you need to perform—a strategy used by many professional and Olympic athletes.

As I read this book, I realized that I had been doing this for years—with math. I had a fearless Statistics professor, Professor Janet Myhre, who led my undergraduate research group. This was my first experience with research, and at first I was so nervous! Every time we tried a different type of regression analysis on our data, I was freaking out. What if it doesn't work? What if I did it wrong? What if... What if... She, on the other hand, was confident and unfazed by the idea of failure or mistakes. If you make a mistake, fix it. If it doesn't work, try something else. If that doesn't work, try something else. You just keep trying until you get something that works.

When I returned years later to get my Master's in Math, I embraced that mentality whenever I started to get flustered. I'd think, *No. Professor Myhre wouldn't be fazed by this. She'd just do it. She'd just figure it out. She'd find a way.* I tapped into her mathematical fearlessness whenever I didn't have it myself, but needed it.

Who would be your math alter ego? If you could show up to your math test as anybody, who would you show up as? What qualities would they have? Would they be prepared? Confident? How would they react in the face of uncertainty?

CRUSH MATH NOW

Choose two of the "Fear Cures" and try them *now*.

STUDY TO BUILD CONFIDENCE

Regardless of the cause of your lack of confidence, here are a few tips to help you study in a way that will build your confidence.

End with easy problems. As a professor, my best classes are the ones when I remember to end on an easier question. We finish up the hardest stuff, review an easier question at the end, and the class leaves feeling confident. My worst classes are the ones that end with everyone frustrated and confused because we ran out of time and ended on a hard problem that we didn't quite finish. Your study sessions likely mimic these emotions. If you end your study session on an easier question, you'll remind yourself that you did learn something and leave more confident. Take an extra couple minutes and look back over the easier questions before you end your study session.

Be on the lookout for curveballs. Every test will have some curveballs, so especially if you have test anxiety, you want to prepare for them. As you go through homework and listen to lectures, keep a lookout for any questions that could be curveballs on the test, such as a particularly hard problem that the teacher spends a lot of time on in class. Or it could be a particularly hard problem that comes up at the end of homework. You'll be less stressed if you track the curveballs that may appear on your next test.

Rewrite excuses as obstacles to overcome. The problem "Math is too hard" can be rewritten as, "Math is hard, but I will figure out how to succeed anyway." The excuse that "I'm just not good at math" can be rewritten as, "Math is a skill that requires practice, and I need to practice more." The excuse "I can't pass because I panic on tests" can be rewritten as "How do I study in a way that allows me to face and learn to power through the panicky feelings I get during tests?" Write down those excuses as problems and get to work solving them.

These are exercises that will get you started on the right path. It'll get you preparing more. It'll get you tackling your homework more confidently. Ultimately, though, the thing that will boost your confidence will be your first big win.

BUILD YOUR CONFIDENCE ON TEST DAY

Here are a few strategies that help students calm down on the day of their exam.

Have a pre-test routine. Have your calculators, pencil, eraser, and whatever else you are allowed to use (notes or formula page if you have an easy teacher) handy. Knowing that you have everything you need will help put your mind at ease.

Do warm-up questions right before your exam. You don't jump into a basketball game without warming up. You wouldn't start a marathon without first stretching. So why does nobody warm up before their math test? It is the marathon of academics, and you must respect it as such. The morning of the exam, make sure you do a few warm-up problems, such as two easy questions that you know for sure will be on the test. It will build your confidence going into the test, and you'll breathe a sigh of relief when you see those first few easy questions on the test.

Write down all formulas as soon as you get the test. Maria was an Algebra student who failed her first test. She left so many problems blank that she didn't have a chance at passing. This particular strategy catapulted her grade to an A. That's right. Not just passing, but an A. She had the highest grade increase in the class. How did she do it? As soon as she got her test, she wrote down every single formula she needed. It turned out that what had held her back was blanking out on the formulas. If she could just get the starting point—the formula—she could figure out the rest. Write down the formulas as soon as you get the test. Then you don't have to worry about forgetting them mid-test.

CRUSH MATH NOW

Pick three or more strategies from this chapter to try out. Write them into your *Crush Math Now Game Plan* and try them out now.

Remember, your confidence won't change overnight. These steps are laying the foundations for your confidence to grow once you get your first big win.

5. WHAT TO DO IF YOU LACK GRIT AND DISCIPLINE

According to the Statistic Brain Research Institute, only 8 percent of people are able to keep their New Year's resolutions. Who are the 8 percent that keep them, and why are they so different from the rest of us? Why are they able to stick with their goals when the other 92 percent of us can't? Because they've developed an important skill: discipline.

Likewise, how do certain people become Navy Seals? By training occasionally, like when they feel like it? By training morning to night for a week, then burning out and quitting? By being wishy-washy about their goals and watching TV? No, they become Navy Seals because they have done the work necessary to get there. How? By developing an important skill: discipline.

Lastly, how do you think certain students get an A in math? By studying occasionally, when they feel like it? By studying morning to night for a few days, then burning out and quitting? By being wishy-washy about their goals and watching TV? No, they become A math students because they have done the work necessary to get there. How? By developing an important skill: discipline.

If you really want to succeed in math, it's important to you, and you believe you can succeed if you do the work, but you just can't bring yourself to do the work, it's likely that the primary thing holding you back is this one skill: discipline.

Thankfully, there are some common reasons for lacking discipline, as well as some simple steps to help you develop the skill of discipline. The reasons include:

Lack of Goals. I know you want to crush math, but you need to get more specific than that. What's the exact grade you need to get on your next assignment? If you don't get that grade, what will happen? What impact will that have on your grade and your future? If you can reach your goals without crushing math, then you need bigger, hairier, more audacious goals. In that case, what you have is not a discipline issue; it's a goals issue. If you lack discipline because you lack big, hairy, audacious goals that you really, really want to accomplish, read Chapter 2, then come back and read this chapter.

Lack of Confidence. If you think, "What's the point of doing the work because it'll just be a waste of time; it's not gonna work, and I'm still gonna fail anyway," you're either not confident in yourself or you're not confident that what you're doing will be effective. Either way, this is not a discipline issue. It is a confidence issue (see Chapter 4) or an issue with studying ineffectively (see Chapter 8). Read the corresponding chapter, and then come back and read this chapter.

Lack of Motivation. If you have discipline in other areas of your life—like when you commit to running at 5 am to train for that marathon, you can actually get up at 5 am to run—but can't get yourself to study math, then you have a motivation issue, not a discipline issue. Think about it. If you cared about math as much as you care about the areas where you do have discipline, you'd be able to do the work. Therefore, you need stronger, more meaningful reasons *why* you need to succeed in math. Without a strong reason why, you'll never do the work. If this is you, read Chapter 3, and then come back to read this chapter.

Procrastination with Poor Time Management Skills. You don't do your homework until the last minute, so sometimes it doesn't get done. You don't study for your test until the last minute, so sometimes you don't study enough. You have enough discipline to study at the last minute, but you have *poor time management skills* that prevent you from succeeding. Personally, I don't think procrastination is a problem. Procrastinate wisely, and you can get the correct amount of work done in a very short period of time. Procrastinate poorly, and you find yourself failing math. There's a fine line between the two, and you must walk it carefully. If your discipline issue boils down to being a procrastinator with a time management issue, read Chapter 9 to learn how to manage your time better. Then, come back to read this chapter.

The Social Stigma of Trying. Often, students lack discipline because they're actually afraid their friends or peers will mock the fact that they're trying. Certain groups of students are just like that. Some students might mock you for being good at math. Others might mock you just for trying. Plus, it's easier or cooler to brush off failure as a lack of caring or lack of trying. It's embarrassing to try and fail. Remember Harper, the surfer/actress/slacker who ultimately was hiding her fear of trying? Throughout high school, she herself had laughed at so many classmates for trying and failing that she was petrified to try herself. Students never want to admit that the social stigma of trying is what's holding them back. As much as it's not cool to try, it's also not cool to care about what other people think. Honestly, sometimes the social dynamics of high school and college can be infuriatingly stupid. If you're caught up in these types of counterproductive friendships, my advice is to not share your attempts to crush math with the people who will mock or judge you. Do the work, make the changes, and only share your journey to crushing math with people who will support and encourage you.

If any of the reasons above pertain to you, read those chapters first. If not, continue reading and try not to get offended.

YOU'RE LAZY

And if you're lazy now, you're setting yourself up for a lifetime of laziness. You've got to crush laziness today.

Let's start by understanding what laziness is because you can be lazy without sitting on the couch and watching TV. *Laziness is not liking to do things that are difficult.* Though you may not like the word "lazy," you might be the kind of person who shies away from things that require effort or persistence. You might shy away from things that make you uncomfortable. You might like to stay in your comfort zone and do things that you know you'll be able to succeed in. This, my friend, is laziness.

Why is it so easy to be lazy? Because we are surrounded by temptation. We are surrounded by things that are easy, distracting and vying for our attention. Netflix. YouTube videos. Instagram and every other app on your phone. All of these are temptations that you give in to when you should be studying math. If you're lazy and distracted by everything under the sun because it's more interesting than math, you lack discipline.

Before we get into strategies to develop discipline, there are a few things you need to understand.

Understand that discipline is the ability to resist temptation. It is the ability to do what you *should* do instead of what you *want* to do. It's the ability to choose a greater long-term payout over a smaller short-term payout. It's choosing to go to the gym and not eat Doritos because of the long-term health and attractiveness benefits over not going to the gym and eating Doritos because that just sounds nice right now. It's the ability to choose studying math and reading this book because in the long run it will make you more successful, smarter, wealthier, and better at problem-solving than everything else in the world that is more interesting and would be more fun than math right now. To make the disciplined decision, you must have a clear sense of the long-term consequences. If you need to, go back to Chapter 2 and fine-tune your goals and game plan. They need to be big and bold. They need to be something you're passionate about. Something awesome enough that you can resist temptation today for that amazing payout tomorrow.

Understand that discipline doesn't mean perfection. Discipline is a pattern or repeated behavior of choosing the thing that you should do. However, you don't need to choose it 100 percent of the time. Don't beat yourself up if you make the wrong decision every once in a while. I've mistakenly eaten the bag of Doritos instead of going to the gym. I've gotten distracted with texting friends when I should have been writing this book. It happens. You must forgive these bumps in the road. Pick yourself up and try again. Discipline is not black and white. It isn't innate. It isn't "you have it or you don't." It is a skill that you practice and become better at over time. So start practicing it today, but don't expect to be perfect. Just pick yourself up when you fall and try again.

Understand that discipline gets harder as the day goes on. I'm never tempted to eat a bag of Doritos and binge watch Netflix first thing in the morning. Why? Because my willpower is at its max. I'm rested and energized and ready to take on the day. But what about at the end of the day, after everything in my chaotic life has pulled me in every direction and exhausted me? Yeah, that's when I'll binge eat Doritos and binge watch Netflix instead of writing this book. At the end of the day, your energy, patience, and willpower are depleted, so if you're trying to develop the discipline to do your math homework at the end of your exhausting day, you're setting yourself up for failure. Discipline gets harder as the day goes on, and it gets near impossible once the sun goes down.

As you read through the following tips, keep these critical facts about discipline in mind. First, discipline is a skill that enables you to resist temptation so that Future You will be awesome. Second, you'll never be perfectly disciplined, so expect to fail and need to pick yourself up occasionally. Third, it's stupid to think you can be disciplined about studying math at the end of the day.

STRATEGIES TO DEVELOP DISCIPLINE

Here are some tips for crushing laziness and developing the discipline to keep your New Year's resolution, become a Navy Seal, or raise your math grade:

Set small goals. A mistake students often make when trying to become disciplined about studying math is setting goals or habits that are bonkers unrealistic. Students tell me that, to pull up their grades, they're making room for a full two hours of math every single day...forever. Seriously?! Are you really going to do two hours of math every single day until the end of time? Is that actually something you want to do? No! Yuck. That is not a sustainable goal, and it's setting you up for failure. For something short-term, like cramming for a test for which you're unprepared, sure, anything goes. But for discipline, for creating habits that stick, start with smaller goals.

Make it your goal to spend one minute a day reading over your goals and game plan. Make your goal to spend five minutes a day quizzing yourself on a certain question type you struggle with. Make it your goal to circle questions you don't know so you can review them later. Small habits you can easily tackle are better than big habits you can't stick with. Set yourself up for success. Write down five mini habits that, if you stuck with them, would have a positive impact on your math grade.

Advertise to yourself. The one small strategy that will make the biggest difference is to read your goals every day. To get into the habit of doing this, attach this habit to one that already exists. Since you brush your teeth every morning, tape your goals next to the bathroom mirror and look at it while you brush your teeth. If you make coffee every morning, tape your goals next to (or on) your coffee maker. Since you look at your phone approximately 75 times per day, make your goals the background or home screen on your phone. The world advertises to you every day, which is why you might subtly think you'll be happier if you have a nicer car, own nicer things, or go to nicer places. You don't need cars advertised to you, though. You need your goals advertised to you, and you must do this yourself. Trust me, if you can build in a way to see your goals automatically throughout the day, your discipline will improve dramatically.

Reward yourself, but also punish yourself. If at the end of every week, my husband and I have met our goals, we treat ourselves to a fun date night. We make it something fun, something different, something exciting that we can look forward to, so that it motivates us. If we don't meet our goals, we pay the babysitter anyway, stay home, and finish our work. Basically, we throw $100 down the drain. We haven't missed our weekly goals once since we started this. It makes us think twice and set goals that are bold, yet realistic. It motivates us to stick to our goals when we'd really just rather veg out or watch TV instead. I encourage you to experiment with a punishment and reward system that works for you. Pair it with an accountability partner, like your boyfriend, girlfriend, spouse, or best friend, and you'll be doubly likely to stick with it.

Analyze and optimize your habits. At the end of each day or week, reflect on the habits you're trying to develop. Just for a minute or two. Think about what worked and what didn't. Which habits are helpful, and which aren't? What motivated you, and what didn't? By taking a minute each day or a couple of minutes each week, you'll consistently fine-tune the habits you're developing, making them better and more in line with your goals, which in turn will make them easier to stick with.

Remove temptations. Dieting was easier before I had kids. I simply didn't keep junk food in the house, so I was never tempted. Once I had kids, at every holiday, birthday party, and soccer game, new, deliciously tempting sweets and treats entered our home. Dieting when surrounded by Girl Scout cookies, fruit snacks, and candy is impossible. It's like an alcoholic trying to stop drinking while keeping her bar fully stocked. It just doesn't work, because you're surrounded by temptation. The same goes for math. You can't develop the discipline to do your math homework if you don't remove the things that tempt you, that distract you, that prevent you from getting your math done. Make a list of the things that distract you the most, and find a way to eliminate them when you do your math homework. Turn off the TV. Silence your phone notifications. Tell your siblings to shut up and leave you alone. Turn off the music that's fun to sing along to. Take down the picture of your boyfriend, so you stop dreaming of him instead of doing math. Sometimes, removing temptation is enough to develop discipline.

Change *when* you study. Willpower, energy, patience, and discipline all decrease throughout the day. Math is important, so you must build time for it into your schedule. The end of the day, when you're exhausted, is the worst—yet most common—time to study math. Here's the thing: We're human. We're not superhuman. Expecting yourself to be able to power through really hard work (i.e. math) when you're exhausted from a long day is not a reasonable expectation for a human. That's what you'd expect out of a superhuman. I know we're bombarded with media images of superheroes who can save the world without showing any of the work that goes into training for that, but don't disillusion yourself! Your problem is *not* needing more "willpower to power through." If you're just too damn tired at the end of the day to do math, don't study math at the end of the day! The end of the day should be saved for things you can do when you're mentally and physically exhausted, such as sleeping, reading, doing easy homework that doesn't require (much) thinking, and just taking a break. Don't save the hard, mentally exhausting work for the end of the day.

Eat the frog. Yup, you read that correctly. Mark Twain once said, "If it's your job to eat a frog, it's best to do it first thing in the morning. And if it's your job to eat two frogs, it's best to eat the biggest one first." If math is your frog—the job you hate and must complete—then do it first. Get it over with, so it doesn't hang over your head, ruining the rest of your day. Get it over with before TV or video games, so you can enjoy those things without having to think about the frog you still have to eat. Get it over with, even before you do your other homework. Do the hard work now, so that you can have guilt-free fun later this evening. Eat the frog and crush math.

Create an "Important Things List." Don't bother stuffing your to-do list with all the random "urgent" things that you have to do. Keep a list of the three most *important* things that you need to get done today. Important meaning crucial to your long-term goals. Important meaning stepping stones to improving Future You. Get those done first. I'll be honest, my life is too busy, and I have zero time for my important goals once the day starts. I have zero time for the stepping stones to Future Me being awesome. Therefore, I get up at 5 am, two hours before everybody else in my house, and I knock everything important off my list before the day begins. Guess what? The important things get done every single day. (If you're really up for a challenge and want to get all your important things done before everyone else starts their day, read *The Miracle Morning* by Hal Elrod. *Crush Math Now* wouldn't exist without it.)

That's it! Pick small habits to focus on. Remove temptation. Do the math first. That's really the key to developing the discipline to crush math. It sounds so simple, but the truth is that developing any skill is difficult and takes time. Recognize that discipline is a skill you are working on, and don't beat yourself up when you fail. Just pick yourself up tomorrow and start anew.

A SPECIAL NOTE ON BURNOUT

The next biggest obstacle to developing discipline is fighting burnout. Whether it's a mid-semester slump or full-blown math burnout, your motivation (and therefore discipline) will take a hit at some point. Plan for it and set up certain things to combat it, like breaks, rewards, and reflection. It's easy to get psyched with new goals and new ideas at the beginning of the semester. It's easy to get psyched up while reading a new book that motivates you and teaches you the "secrets" to crushing math. The hardest part is sticking with it. Inevitably, at some point in the semester, everyone burns out. How do you fight burnout? How do you overcome it? How do you succeed despite it?

First, you need to understand what student burnout is and what causes it. You burn out when you are exhausted. You've been busy and stressed, studying day in and day out. You feel overwhelmed. You suddenly lack the motivation to power through. You're exhausted—physically, mentally and emotionally. It's all just too much. Burnout can even come with feelings of depression, hopelessness, resentment or simply a huge "I don't care anymore." In today's competitive world, with so much expected of students, burnout isn't just possible; without proper precautions, it's probable. Instead of ignoring the possibility of burnout, and expecting to "power through" if it shows up, it's best to plan ahead, anticipate it, and combat it.

Here are habits to help combat math burnout:

Take a Break. This is not optional. You must build breaks into your schedule. When I was in high school, my sister and I would go to a concert almost once a quarter. It was fun, exhilarating, and something I'd look forward to from the moment we bought the tickets. In college, my friends and I would venture off campus for various trips once a quarter—skiing, concerts, conferences, or just a girls' weekend away. Today, my husband and I get away from the craziness of raising three kids once a quarter for a quiet, kid-free weekend, complete with a nice hotel and grown-up restaurants. Quarterly breaks, as well as daily, weekly, and monthly breaks, are crucial to staying on track the rest of the time.

Reflect at Bedtime. Many successful people have a bedtime routine that revolves around reflecting on how their day went and on how they're living their lives. Some people pray. Others read. Yet others meditate. Benjamin Franklin would ask himself, "What good have I done today?" Other good questions to ask yourself are: *What did I learn today? What steps did I take toward my goals today?* My bedtime routine is simple. At the end of my life, I want to have no regrets. I want to be able to say that, if I had a chance to live my life over again, I'd do it exactly the same way. At the end of the day, I ask myself: If I had to do today over again, would I do it exactly the same?

Begin with the End in Mind. Each day, think of who you want to be when you graduate. Do you want to be someone who crushed math? Someone who took specific classes for specific reasons and accomplished their goals? Someone who learned to finish what they begin? The kind of person who is setting themselves up to live the life of their dreams? Everything you do today determines the kind of person that you are tomorrow. Think about who you want to be when you graduate, then do what you must today to become that person.

CRUSH MATH NOW

Pick the three strategies from this chapter that you think will have the biggest impact on your grade, write them in your *Crush Math Now Game Plan,* and start them now.

6. WHAT TO DO IF YOU'RE STRUGGLING TO SUCCEED ON YOUR OWN

You're trying to figure this out on your own. Maybe you have no family to help and guide you, or maybe asking them for help is the last thing you'd ever want to do. You've had minimal interactions with teachers or tutors at school and wouldn't consider them a support system. Your friends either don't care about crushing math or simply don't know how. Either way, you're isolated and don't know who to turn to or how to reach out for help.

The bad news is that it takes a village to crush math. The good news is that your village can be small. It only takes a couple of people. The even better news is that there's an army of people out there waiting to help you succeed; it's just a matter of figuring out how and when to utilize them.

Here are the three people you need in your village:

1. **An Expert.** You need one person who can teach you the math, who has crushed math already, who can clarify the things that are confusing, and who

can help you build your skill set. This isn't necessarily your teacher though. It could be a parent, friend, another teacher, or a tutor.

2. **A Champion.** You need one person who believes in you, who will encourage you to challenge yourself and believes that you are capable of great things. This person may not be able to help you with the math itself, but they believe that you can and will crush math.

3. **A Rock.** You need one person to turn to when the going gets tough. One person who has grit, is mentally tough, and can lead you by example. One person who will help you pick yourself up when you fail or fall.

The cool thing is, if you have someone who encapsulates all three of these qualities, you can even get by with a village of one.

And, FYI, this is one of those parts of the book that doesn't just pertain to math. For any big, hairy, audacious goal you aspire to, you can reach your goal by finding an *expert* to show you how to get there, a *champion* who believes you can get there, and a *rock* who will help you pick youself up when you have setbacks.

As you read through the rest of the chapter, keep this in mind. You don't need to be BFFs with every math student and math teacher. You just need to build your village of three.

Now, if you only need three people, why is it so hard to find help? Because of the following five problems:

1. You want to succeed without help.
2. You have a bad math teacher.

3. You don't utilize your school's tutoring center.
4. Your family and friends aren't math people.
5. You're too introverted to ask for help.

Don't worry. These problems are not insurmountable. No matter where you are today, you can overcome these problems, build your village, and succeed in math.

PROBLEM 1: YOU WANT TO SUCCEED WITHOUT HELP.

Suppose you sucked at soccer and wanted to be awesome at it, but you didn't know a single person who was good at soccer. The first thing you would probably do is try to figure it out on your own. The Internet is filled with videos and tutorials you can learn from, and how hard could it be to learn to kick a ball around?

Now, suppose you were able to master some soccer skills on your own but struggled to figure others out or, even worse, you learned to do certain things the wrong way or didn't realize there were other things you needed to learn. You'd go out to play soccer only to be one of the worst players on the team. Obviously, something isn't working, but you either don't know what it is or you don't know how to fix it. You've gone as far as you can, succeeded as much as you can, in isolation. What would be the next step, if you were truly dedicated to being awesome at soccer? Do you continue to persevere in stubborn isolation? At what point do you change this strategy?

Now, suppose your team has a coach, a person who has decided that of all the jobs in the world, the one they wanted to dedicate their lives to was teaching people to play soccer. Will you reach your goal faster if you avoid your coach like the plague, hoping they either don't notice you or forget who you are?

Next, suppose your coach holds office hours for the sole purpose of helping the soccer players who need some extra help. Will you reach your goal faster if you avoid your coach's office hours at all costs?

Suppose some of the other players on your soccer team are really talented soccer players. Will you reach your goal faster if you avoid them at all costs and instead ask your non-soccer-playing friends and family for advice about improving your game?

Lastly, suppose your soccer league offers a training center where the best soccer players, who have been selected specifically for their teaching abilities, hang out, with the sole purpose of helping struggling soccer players succeed. Will you reach your goal faster if you avoid this training center—designed and funded specifically to help you—like the plague?

No! Yet, for some reason, this is exactly the strategy that struggling math students take. I know it makes you uncomfortable to reach out for help, but ultimately, to be successful, you must get used to doing the things that make you uncomfortable. As Brian Tracy, a kickass writer on motivation and success, says, "Move out of your comfort zone. You can only grow if you are willing to feel awkward and uncomfortable when trying something new."

So, this is my challenge to you: Move out of your comfort zone. Ask your math teacher for help. Go to your teacher's office hours. Ask the best math students, not other failing or struggling math students, for advice. Go to your school's math center and ask for help. Do all these things, despite how uncomfortable it makes you feel because that is how you will succeed.

If you take math long enough, you'll eventually hit a level of math where you can't figure it out on your own and you need help. It takes a village. Not a village of Internet tutorials and other failing math students. It takes a village of three specific people and one of those people needs to have already figured out how to succeed in math. From my experience, this is obvious to everyone *except* students who are struggling in math.

Now, at this point, all the problems with your village are likely at the forefront of your mind. You may feel you don't have a village of experts at your disposal; you have a village of idiots! You have a bad teacher. Your class has A+ math students who are condescending or unapproachable. Your school has a tutoring center filled with unhelpful tutors who leave you *more* confused instead of enlightened. Trust me, these problems are not insurmountable. Let's look at some specific solutions to these problems.

PROBLEM 2: YOU HAVE A BAD MATH TEACHER.

In my many years as a math teacher, I only had one really bad math teacher. We'd ask her a question and then spend the rest of class watching her make every error in the book, struggling to solve one simple problem. She didn't know how to use a calculator. She didn't understand enough math to calculate our grades. That all would've been forgivable if she at least cared, but she hated us. Not in an "I'm strict for your own good" way, but in an "I don't care about you or if you succeed" way. She was the worst.

Now, in retrospect, I feel bad for her. She didn't understand what she was getting herself into when she signed up to teach math. She didn't realize how ill-prepared she was and she couldn't figure out how to improve. But at the time, none of that mattered. All I knew was that I had a bad math teacher and I had to figure out how to succeed despite her.

The truth is, though, that most teachers are not that bad.

Struggling math students typically wildly exaggerate how bad their teachers are. As a former math tutor, I can tell you that every single student who struggles in math is convinced it's because they have a bad math teacher. As a former math student, I can tell you that every single one of my professors was flawed in some way, even my absolute favorites. Ultimately, it doesn't matter if your teacher is bad. This is just another obstacle to crushing math that you must overcome.

To overcome a bad teacher, focus on our teacher's strengths, instead of weaknesses. It's unlikely that your teacher will be your expert, your champion *and* your rock. If your teacher can't explain the material, then don't make them your go-to expert. Find someone else. If your teacher doesn't believe in you, don't expect them to be your champion. Succeed despite them and prove them wrong. If your teacher doesn't offer support when you're struggling, find someone who does.

Here are some common complaints I hear about math teachers and my advice for each situation:

Your teacher is awkward, unapproachable, or intimidating. Many math professors, myself included, are a special kind of quirky. Often, I find myself in conversations among normal people thinking, "Could I be any more awkward? Did I really just say that out loud to another human being? " Yup, that's the inner dialogue of many a mathematician. We are not known for our social skills. If your teacher is awkward, unapproachable, or intimidating, assume it's because they never quite mastered the eloquent social skills you possess, cut them some slack, and ask them questions anyway. You just might be surprised by how helpful they can be.

Your teacher is confusing or doesn't explain the material clearly. This teacher should not be the expert you go to learn the material. Yes, you'll have to sit through class and you should still use that time to learn the material to the best of your ability. However, if you can, find another teacher, tutor or parent to be the expert you go to for help learning the material. If all else fails and you need to ask your confusing teacher questions, ask them very specific questions, write down their explanations, and then read it back to them to ensure you got the message correctly.

Your teacher is unorganized or forgetful. This doesn't affect their ability to answer your questions or provide support. If that's your biggest complaint, consider yourself lucky.

Your teacher doesn't care. Some teachers just don't care. Maybe they're jaded from years of jackass students making excuses and being dumb. Maybe life beat them down —you know, bills to pay, cars to buy, student loans to pay off— that stuff will wear anyone down. Maybe they wanted to be the guy in *Moneyball* and are pissed they got stuck teaching. Oh, the things they could've been! Get over it. Use them as a resource for learning the material, but don't expect them to be a mentor for moral support.

Your teacher doesn't understand your specific situation. In case you didn't notice, your teacher has more than one student and their life doesn't revolve around you. [FYI— it's not just your math teacher. Nobody else's life revolves around you and that kind of thinking is something you should have outgrown somewhere between being a toddler and now.] Ask yourself, "Can this teacher still help me figure out the math, even if they're not caught up in what's going on in my world?" The answer is probably yes.

Your teacher's teaching style isn't conducive to how you learn best. If this is you, you're getting really over-the-top nitpicky and I have a wake-up call for you. It's your job to adapt to your teacher's teaching style, not their job to adapt to your learning style. There are 30, possibly 100, students in your class. It's literally impossible for them to adjust to everyone's "learning style."

Almost every math teacher has flaws. The difference between students who crush math and those who struggle is that students who crush math don't care if their teacher is bad. They suck it up and figure out how to overcome a bad math teacher. They find a way to utilize their teachers' strengths instead of complaining about their weaknesses.

Now that you understand the above, let's figure out how to utilize the most unapproachable or unhelpful teacher. There are three primary ways to do this:

1. Talk to your teacher before/during/after class. This is ideal if you don't have time outside of class.
2. Go to office hours. This is where you will get the most help.
3. Email your teacher. This is the easiest and least intimidating form of communication.

As a bonus, if you regularly email and go to office hours, you might develop a strong enough relationship with your math teacher that you can ask them for a college, grad school, or job recommendation. Nothing says smart like a recommendation from a math teacher!

PROBLEM 3: YOU DON'T UTILIZE YOUR SCHOOL'S TUTORING CENTER.

The problem here is that struggling math students either have never set foot in their school's math tutoring center or went once, didn't find it helpful, and never tried it again. Often, struggling math students go for the first time during finals week—the one week of the semester when the tutoring center is packed and might even have a line. Don't go then. Go earlier in the semester, when it's empty and tutors are sitting around waiting for somebody, *anybody* to come in.

The second problem is that struggling math students go to the tutoring center looking for an expert to better explain the math concepts, when what they are really struggling with is math anxiety or discipline or motivation. What they really ought to be looking for is a champion or a rock. They leave complaining that they didn't find what they were looking for because they went in looking for the wrong person.

Make sure you go in looking for the right person. What do you lack most — an expert, a champion, or a rock? If you need an expert, you're in the right place. Math center tutors are hired specifically for their ability to explain mathematics in a clear and helpful way. If you need a champion or a rock (which are just as important), you need to go in looking specifically for that. You might need to talk to a few more tutors before finding one that works, but you can still find one.

Here are a few additional benefits of school tutoring centers that are often overlooked:

It's free. I don't think students realize how lucky they are. When I was a college student tutoring math, I charged $60/hour. Post-college, my rate was $120/hour, and, when I worked at and trained tutors for Kaplan Test Prep, they charged students upwards of $225/hour for my tutoring services. For every hour you're spending in your school's math tutoring center, you're saving yourself $60—$225/hour.

It's at your school. You're already on campus for class, so you don't have to travel anywhere. Just walk over after class one day and check it out. It should take all of five minutes to find and all of twenty minutes to ask a question that will save you two hours of time trying to figure out on your own.

It has experts. Exceptional students, teachers, or professional tutors—you know, experts who know the answers to your problems—work at the tutoring center. They don't employ people who don't have something to offer.

Someone can help you. It might not be the first tutor you ask for help. It might not be the second either, but odds are it'll be the third or fourth. Here's the thing: Even if you were paying a math tutor $120/hour, you might still have to try a few out to find the one that works best for you. So don't complain, "Oh, woe is me! If only I could afford an expensive math tutor!" No! You'd go through the same process with expensive tutors: You'd either complain and blame a tutor for not helping, or you'd keep at it until you find someone who does help.

You need to take advantage of the resources available to you and figure out a way to make them work to your benefit. *Someone* at your math center can figure out your problems. *Someone* at your math center can explain things in a way that makes sense. *Someone* at your math center can help with whatever random math class you're taking. No excuses. Find a way to utilize your school's math center. It will save you time and a small fortune.

PROBLEM 4: YOUR FAMILY AND FRIENDS AREN'T MATH PEOPLE.

A very wise man, Jim Rohn, once said, "You are the average of the five people you spend the most time with." If the people you spend the most time with are rich, happy, successful, fun people, you'll most likely be rich, happy, successful, and fun. In other words, choose your friends wisely.

If the five people you spend the most time with are failing math, you'll most likely fail math too. I am not saying that you should ditch your friends willy-nilly and replace them with successful ones. Life is not black and white. It's a lot of grey area, so navigate the social stuff carefully, but wisely. However, if you want to get an A in Math, find at least one person to study with, who is already getting an A in math, and you'll naturally gravitate toward his or her good habits.

The bottom line is that it's in your best interest to have at least one friend who is successful in math or who is at least willing to make that journey with you.

The most successful people in the world do not reach success in complete isolation. They have many people who have supported them on their journey to success, and these people did not magically appear. They were found. The friendships were cultivated over time. They were worked on. They were mutual. They were helpful. Successful people have, through years of practice, figured out how to surround themselves with the best people. To get you started, here are five types of relationships to help you succeed in both math and life: mentors, classmates, accountability partners, mastermind groups, and mentees.

Mentors: Tutors and teachers are the easiest people to add to your circle because they're paid to make themselves available to help you! All you have to do is take advantage of the resources available to you. Just go to office hours or your school's math center. Done!

Classmates: Who are the most approachable A students in your class? The ones who will answer your questions and help you out, rather than just make you feel bad about yourself? These are the students you want to sit near and ask questions of. These are the students you want to study with.

Accountability Partners: Studious friends make great accountability partners—people who hold you accountable for showing up to study. They don't necessarily have to be in your math class or be able to help you with math. They can work on their own classwork while you work on yours.

Mastermind Group: Do you know how millionaires figure out how to become millionaires? Or how billionaires figure out how to become billionaires? By getting involved in mastermind groups! Mastermind groups bring together the smartest, toughest, most successful problem solvers. The people obsessed with the mantra to "do the thing you think you cannot do." And they do it. They work together and figure it out. They support each other. They teach each other and learn from each other. They solve problems together. They grow together, and they succeed together. Forget study groups. Create your own mastermind group.

Mentees: On the other side of the spectrum, if you want to get better at math, be the mentor and help someone else succeed by tutoring them in math. It'll solidify your foundations, help you learn to talk articulately about mathematics, develop your listening and communication skills, and improve your confidence in your math abilities. It's not just a win for your mentee, it's a win for you, too.

PROBLEM 5: YOU ARE TOO INTROVERTED TO ASK FOR HELP.

I know that despite the many, many benefits of building a support system, some of you will simply refuse. You'd rather fail than ask for help. You'd rather study an extra five hours on your own than spend ten minutes visiting your teacher in office hours. If this is you, and you really won't give any of the above suggestions a try, here are a few tips just for you:

Forget in-person study groups. If your initial reaction to meeting up with classmates to study is "heck no!" then forget in-person study groups. Instead, find classmates or friends you can text questions to. This is can be just as effective as meeting in person.

Email the teacher. Each semester, at least one of my top students is an introvert who emails me. One of my top College Algebra students was an introvert. He never once came to my office hours. He'd barely look at people in class, and it would never occur to him ever to talk to a classmate for any reason. However, he was smart enough to know when he needed help. When the class got tough, he emailed me questions.

Find alternate math books. If you're in Calculus III and your book simply makes things more confusing, check out other Calculus III books from the library and find one that clarifies things. I've taken several classes from professors who were writing their own textbooks, which meant everyone was studying from an unedited, semi-completed textbook—Not the most helpful resource. Right now, as I think about the textbooks I'm required to teach from, honestly, the content and quality vary. Some chapters do a great job, others not so much. Especially if you're a student who doesn't want to utilize resources like office hours or the math center, looking at different textbooks, with different explanations of the material you're covering, can very much make up for a lacking support system. Textbooks also provide more in-depth answers and solutions than a simple Google search.

CRUSH MATH NOW

1. Find a problem that you missed and didn't understand on your last homework, quiz, or test. Ask your teacher for help, either in class, in office hours, or via email.
2. Find out the hours and location of your school's math center. Pick one homework problem to ask them, and go ask the next time you're on campus. Remember: the first step is always the hardest.

3. Build a support system of three people. Brainstorm every person you know or know of who could help you crush math. Of those, pick the most approachable and/or helpful. Ask them for help. Now.

7. WHAT TO DO IF YOU HAVE AN EMERGENCY OR PERMANENT OBSTACLE

Personal problems that prevent you from crushing math fall into two categories: *emergencies* and *permanent obstacles*. Emergencies are temporary and urgent, and they might require you to put your goal of crushing math on hold. Whether you resort to asking your professor for an extension or even dropping the class, the emergency must be taken care of first. Obstacles, however, are permanent problems. Even if you postpone taking math, the obstacle will still be there waiting for you. Which category does your problem fall into?

In any given semester, I might have a student who fails or withdraws from my class for one of the following reasons: a learning disability, the passing away of a parent, a job loss that resulted in them being homeless (or nearly), a break-up or other event that triggered their depression or drug addiction, or a medical emergency. On the other hand, every semester, I also have students who have passed and crushed math despite these exact same problems. Whether or not your problem is an emergency or an obstacle depends on you and your particular situation.

EMERGENCIES

If you have an emergency, then reach out for help and take care of your emergency immediately. What constitutes an emergency? If we go by Maslow's hierarchy of human needs, you need clothes on your back, a place to sleep, and food to eat. You need to be safe. You need to be physically and mentally healthy. If any of these needs are not met, do what you must to meet those needs now, and then come back and crush math.

Here's a list of people you can contact for help:

1. The Police Department (If you fear for your physical safety, call the police. They're the experts here and can help you in these extreme circumstances.)
2. A friend, parent, or sibling you can trust
3. Your school's counseling center
4. Your school's student services center
5. Your doctor, therapist, or another health professional
6. Your teacher (Honestly, math teachers are not trained on this stuff, but over the years many of us have helped students find the correct resources to overcome many of these problems. If your math teacher—or any other teacher—is someone you can reach out to, ask for help.)

There are so many other people who could go on this list, too. The point here is to take 100 percent responsibility for your situation, your safety, and your well-being.

In Chapter 6, I discuss how many students try out the math center once, don't find any help, then give up and never ask for help again. My advice there, which is the same advice here, is to not give up so easily. If the first counselor or friend or teacher or police officer you reach out to isn't helpful, try a second. If the second isn't helpful, find a third. Don't fixate on people's flaws or a flawed support system. They will always be imperfect and no one will magically appear at your door and fix these emergencies or obstacles. You must be the hero. You must be your own savior. You must be the one who will overcome the problems you face.

PERMANENT OBSTACLES

On the emergency side of the spectrum, students deal with one-time extreme situations that throw them off course. On the other side of the spectrum are students dealing with permanent obstacles. These can include the following:

1. You have a learning disability.
2. English is your second language.
3. You have kids.
4. You work full-time and are in school full-time.
5. You are an adult returning to school after many years.

These are permanent obstacles, and you can't put math off permanently. You'll have to conquer math, despite the obstacle. I'll discuss each of these one by one, but remember two important things that are relevant to all of these problems:

1. Be your own hero. There are no fairy godmothers or knights in shining armor who magically fix everything or rescue you. You must do it yourself.

2. You're not the first. You're not the first math student with a learning disability. Or the first math student who is a single parent trying to keep a roof over their babies' heads. Or the first adult returning to school after decades. Others have come before you. Others just like you have crushed math. I promise you that no matter what your situation is, people in your exact same situation or worse have crushed math, and you can too. It might be the hardest thing you've ever done in your life, but you can do it, and it will be worth it.

PERMANENT PROBLEM 1: YOU HAVE A LEARNING DISABILITY.

As a heads up, I have no formal training on working with students with disabilities. My experiences have been extremely random, but also extremely positive. I think if you approach math and learning disabilities with optimism and an open mind, you'll find the solutions you need.

Whenever possible, I like to think of learning disabilities not as disabilities, but as *learning differently*. For example, I once taught a student named Ashkin. He had a traumatic brain injury, which impaired his vision, his ability to write, and his ability to transition new information from his short-term to long-term memory. He'd been stuck in a vicious cycle of failing and repeating math for a while.

Then, we started experimenting. We discovered that he needs larger printed tests, so he can see the questions and has room to write in very large print. We discovered that taking his tests at the Disabled Students Programs and Services made his anxiety worse than taking the exam in class. We discovered that the repeated practice that students were getting in home-work was not enough for him to commit the information to his long-term memory, so he needed much more repeated practice. He can still learn the material. He's not incapable of learning it. He just learns it differently. If everyone were just like him, tests would be given in bigger fonts on larger papers, and the homework would emphasize more daily repetition of exercises, instead of one-time homework assignments on each topic.

Just because math isn't taught or tested a specific way at school doesn't mean that your way of learning is worse or wrong. It just means it's different and it's up to you to figure out how you learn best.

I know you're thinking, *But that's not me! My learning disability just sucks. It's the reason I'm not succeeding, and I've tried and tried and tried. I still flip numbers, and I always will because I'm dyslexic. I still can't remember what the math steps are, and I'll never get it because I'm ADHD. Or, I understand the math, but I'll still always fail because inevitably a mood swing will always hit during midterms because I'm bipolar. Or, I can't figure it out because I have so many different disabilities that, while I believe I could overcome one or maybe two, I couldn't possibly overcome the many different disabilities I've been cursed with.* I hear you. And I'm not saying that learning disabilities don't suck. They do. Just like all obstacles. What I'm saying is that they are obstacles, just like anything else that stands in the way of crushing math. They are problems, and like all problems, they have a solution. You just need to find it.

So, let's find *your* solution. Here are several powerful strategies to get you started.

Do a brain dump. Write down on paper every single way your disability is preventing you from crushing math. Get as specific as possible. If you fail tests, why? If you don't get homework done, why? Set a timer for five minutes, and write out everything you can think of. Force yourself to keep writing, because the longer you write, the deeper you'll get into your underlying problems. If not being able to write is part of your learning disability, dictate it. No excuses anymore. If exercises in this book are ever given in a way that doesn't work for you, you can no longer say "I can't." Instead, you must now ask yourself, "How can I?"

Rephrase problems as questions. Take the biggest problems from your brain dump and turn them into questions. That's right. You will no longer think, "I can't succeed because of my learning disability." From now on, you will think, and I want you to write this down, "How can I crush math, even though I learn differently?" or "How do I crush math, even though I have [insert learning disability here]?" Okay, take a second and put your question on paper. Did you do it? Yes? Good job! It might seem like a small step, but you'll see soon enough how big a difference that actually makes.

Brainstorm nine solutions. What are nine things that you could try to learn differently or take tests differently? Here's where you get creative and must think outside the box. For example, on the last midterm I gave, one of my students who is both dyslexic and ADHD was struggling to simplify expressions. I had her circle the x-terms and box the y-terms on every single problem. Then, I had her go through and combine all of the circled terms on every single problem. Then I had her go through and combine the boxed terms on every single problem. The process of circling and boxing terms helped her from mixing up the x's and y's. The process of doing the same step on every problem, instead of each problem individually, helped her focus and not get the steps jumbled together. I literally want you to think about the problems you get wrong and brainstorm different ways to do them. Remember, the way you might learn best is not necessarily the way math is taught in class. So pretend it's a blank slate. What way would you best learn the material? What way would you best study? It's different for everyone, and you must find your unique best way.

If you're not used to brainstorming different solutions, I know it can be easy to give up and say, "I don't know." You have to fight against that. If you can't come up with solutions now, come back later today and brainstorm. Or sit down with a parent, teacher, or someone with the same learning disability and brainstorm. I'm not saying it's going to be easy, but I am saying that if you try enough different things, you'll find a way to succeed. Here are some potential solutions from my experience going through this with my students:

Experiment quickly. There is no such thing as trying too many different things. Dylan, my dyslexic student from Chapter 1, found what worked after experimenting with dozens upon dozens of strategies. Every semester, I meet new students with learning disabilities who have never tried different strategies! Never! It boggles my mind! If your situation is different than your classmates, then, of course, you'll need different strategies to succeed. Experiment quickly until you find what works for you.

Look for wildly out-of-the-box solutions. Don't give up. Instead, look for more innovative and out-of-the-box solutions. What was the strategy that worked for Dylan in Chapter 1? Reading the math questions upside down! I never in a million years would have started off with that strategy. We never in a million years would have found the solution if we had stopped experimenting after the first dozen failures.

I had another student, Rafael, who had failed College Algebra multiple times. The thing that helped him pass? Having someone read the test problems to him and write out his work for him as he dictated it. Yet another student got permission to work at his own pace—being allowed to make up work and quizzes when his bipolar mood swings hit. There are so many different solutions, and often the ones that work require wildly out-of-the-box thinking. Be brave and think outside the box.

Use every advantage in your arsenal to win. If you're allowed extra time or a notetaker or a calculator or a computer or anything that might help you, use them. If you have to jump through some hoops, get a doctor's note, or seek your teacher's permission to get accommodations that you know will help you more, jump through the hoops and make it happen. If you can afford a private tutor to help, use one. If you can get your homework done in half the time working one-on-one with a tutor at the math center every day, do it. If you have to research teachers to pick the one who is willing to print a test in extra large font for you, do the research.

Understand that not every accommodation that's offered to you is helpful. I had an SAT Math student with ADHD who was given extended time on the SAT. What helped him? *Not* using the extended time. Learning to fly through the test as quickly as possible was more helpful than extended time. Another student, Ashkin, who needed his exams in large print, also qualified for extended time and a "quiet" testing environment, if he took his exam at the Disabled Students Programs and Services office, so he took his exam there. I went to see if he had any questions and found him in a tiny, cramped, messy office that was making him claustrophobic and aggravated his anxiety. Just because an accommodation is offered doesn't mean that it will actually help you or that you need to use it.

Just ask. Nearly every semester, I have a student with a learning disability who is struggling. They don't do well on their first quiz or test, and we sit down to talk about what's going on. Typically, there's a small change that they know could help, but they're trying to get by without asking for it. Nothing bad can come from asking! The worst that can happen is that your teacher says no. The best that can happen is they allow you an accommodation that will increase your likelihood of success or offer an even better option. Always ask. If you're too nervous to ask in person, write an email similar to the following and attach verification from a doctor.

Dear Professor,

I wanted to let you know that I have the learning disabilities dyslexia and ADHD. I was wondering, if it's possible, for me to have two additional accommodations on the next exam: headphones to listen to white noise (which will help me concentrate) and a calculator (to help me reduce errors on the basic calculations that I mix up). I know these are not typically permitted, but they would be a huge help and, I think, could make the difference between me succeeding and getting mixed up in tiny calculations that aren't the focus of the test. Thank you so much for considering my request.

Warmly,

Allison

The general template for this is:

Dear Mr./Mrs. [Professor's name],

I wanted to let you know that I have the learning disability [specific learning disability]. I was wondering if I could possibly [insert accommodation you're requesting] on my next [quiz/test/assignment]. I think it'll make a huge difference because [reason#1]. In addition, [reason #2]. It would be a tremendous help and, I think, could be the difference between me succeeding and not succeeding. Thank you so much for considering my request.

Warmly,

[Your name]

Understand that not all of your problems are due to your learning disability. This might be a hard one for you to hear. In my experience, just as students without disabilities blame legitimate mistakes on careless errors, students with learning disabilities tend to blame those same mistakes on their learning disabilities. In all fairness, it's often very difficult to tell the reason for the error. Did you make that mistake because you legitimately forgot the order of operations in a really long, complicated problem where anyone could make that error, or because of dyslexia? Of course, you know the order of operations, therefore it must be your learning disability! Not necessarily. This is a mistake that any student could make, and if you're chalking it up to your learning disability, then you're not tackling the problem head-on. My advice is to err on the side of caution. When in doubt, assume your mistakes are due to *not* knowing the material as well as you think or having foundations that are weaker than you think, rather than your learning disability.

PERMANENT PROBLEM 2: ENGLISH IS YOUR SECOND LANGUAGE.

If you're learning math, while simultaneously learning English, you are my hero! That is truly a difficult challenge to take on and the less English you know the bigger the challenge. In my Prealgebra class, I have students from around the world with varying levels of math foundations and English fluency. These students have taught me the following: If you have enough courage to (1) move to a different country where you don't speak the language and (2) jump right into a math class taught in that language, you have the motivation, grit, and discipline necessary to succeed in anything and you absolutely have what it takes to crush math. The good news is that there are only three primary obstacles that stand between you and success. The bad news is that it takes a lot of work to overcome them.

Solving word problems. For word problems, my advice is to (1) study them obsessively, even if it's not required, and (2) focus on keywords. Most math word problems have a few keywords that tell you what to do. In Prealgebra, for example, you'll want to memorize every single keyword that tells you to divide. Quotient, divided by, equal groups, shared equally, distribute, cut up, half, and quarter are all common keywords that tell you to divide. Your teacher may assume that you know these, so if you don't it's up to you to get up to speed and learn them on your own. This may require making flashcards for keywords, finding resources beyond your textbook, or expanding beyond your circle of friends who are also learning English and studying with people who speak English fluently.

Understanding what you need to do and when. Second, make sure you understand what your teacher is asking of you. If you can't understand them, ask them to slow down. Kindly explain that English is your second language and that it would help you if they could speak slower. If you still can't understand them, ask a second time, try asking them to write it down, or ask another student to translate for you. Don't make assumptions about what your teacher is saying. Seek clarification instead.

I start my first class of each semester super excited about all the things we'll learn. I try to reign in my enthusiasm, but sometimes I can't, and, in an attempt to give everyone a "big picture" feel for all the awesome math we'll be covering, I can go off on tangents, talking quickly and excitedly. It's not a burden or annoyance, when a student asks me to slow down. It's immensely helpful. If you don't speak up, your teacher won't know that they need to slow down or be more clear. Believe me, your honesty is appreciated.

Working with new notation. Third, math notation is not standardized throughout the world, so the math notation that you grew up with may be different than what you'll see in class. Just because the notation is different doesn't mean that you're not already familiar with the concept. If you've already learned a concept (but with different notation), you're not learning the concept from scratch. You're simply learning a new way of writing or portraying something you already know. Look for patterns. If something feels familiar, it probably is.

If English is your second language, it's important to tackle these problems head-on and make time to study the language side of mathematics. I had a student once, who had taken Calculus in China, but didn't speak any English. He knew the math, but not the language, and was adamant that he could succeed without learning the English language side of mathematics. Did he know the math? Absolutely. Did he fail his Prealgebra final? Unfortunately, yes.

PERMANENT PROBLEM 3: YOU HAVE KIDS.

If you're a parent and are in school full-time, then your obstacle is an insane life. Stick with it. It'll be worth it in the long run. I found out I was pregnant during the first month of my Master's in Mathematics program. At the time, I thought the hardest thing in the world was trying to juggle working and learning math while battling morning sickness—which isn't necessarily just in the morning. For me, it was 24/7 for several months. Some days I'd throw up before class. Other days, after class. There were a few times when I had to leave right in the middle of class, throw up, then come back and finish taking notes. Fun times.

Now, that was nothing compared to the second year of my Master's, when I was, for the first time ever, trying to keep a newborn baby alive. I was petrified that she might choke on her own spit, inhale carbon monoxide despite the carbon monoxide detector in her room, or just spontaneously combust. When I was nursing, I'd pump milk in the bathroom stalls between classes—not weird at all! I showed up for late-night math reviews at the library lugging a sleeping newborn in a car seat. I remember the desperation and the exhaustion and the chaos like it was yesterday. I remember the moments when I thought it was too hard and too exhausting and just *too much*. And every single time I thought it was too hard to carry on, do you know what I told myself? It'll be worth it in the long run. And you know what? It totally is.

The biggest piece of advice I can give to a parent who's in school is to remind yourself why you're there. Imagine Future You. What life do you envision *in the long run*? Who is the Future You that you want raising your daughter or son and guiding them through the hard times of their life? It's the Future You who crushes math despite how bonkers-insane school gets when you're a parent.

Imagine Future You vividly. Imagine Future You frequently. Imagine Future You every time you think about giving up and every time you think you're too tired to go to class or study or take that exam. They say that 90 percent of success is just showing up. That's true for parenting, life, and math. There will be days when your biggest hurdle will be just showing up.

No matter how hard it gets or how tired you get, *just keep showing up*.

As I reflect back on juggling school with raising my daughter, here are a few things I did that helped and a few things that I wish I'd know because it would've helped.

Develop a support system. Parents often go through school alone. They feel older than classmates and aren't on campus enough. But remember—just as it takes a village to raise your kids, it can take a village to pass a hard math class. If you don't already have a village, start building one. Who are parents you admire and can learn from? Who are parents you can team up with to succeed? During my Master's, I became friends with a mom who was also in school and who had a son the same age as my daughter. I would drive to her apartment, and we'd alternate studying and watching the kids. Some days, I would watch the kids for two hours while she studied, and then she'd watch the kids for two hours while I studied. Other days, she would have something more urgent, and she'd study for the full four hours while I watched the kids or vice versa. Your parenting support system is just as crucial to your success as your math support system.

You don't have to be perfect. I went into motherhood with a bonkers unrealistic idea of how together I'd be. I thought I'd be as fun and laid-back as I was before having a baby. I thought I'd just naturally be an awesome mom, raising my kid with rocket-science precision. I thought I'd be the top math student in my program. And I thought I'd do it all without any help. It seems crazy as I write this, but that's actually what I thought and I got really down on myself when I wasn't meeting those wildly unrealistic expectations. I was so incredibly far from perfect, but that's okay. You don't have to be perfect. You don't have to be as fun as you were before kids, or the most awesome parent on the planet, or the top student, or get through school without any help. Cut yourself some slack. The fact that you're juggling math with raising kids is awesome enough. Don't worry about being perfect.

Show your kids how to succeed. Actions speak louder than words, right? Especially if your kids are older, crushing math is a great way to show them how to succeed. Show them it's not a simple task. It's hard, it's a struggle, and sometimes you fail, but you pick yourself up, learn from it, and persevere. There's no better way to teach your kids to be that kind of person than to be it yourself. One of my students is a mother of two. When her family immigrated to the United States, her children were college-aged and struggled with the transition. They didn't think they could succeed in college here, so they didn't try. How did she change that? *She* went to college. As soon as she made the jump, they followed in her footsteps. She would get so excited when she got 100 percent on a test because she knew it would push her own kids to work harder. Actions, my friend, speak louder than words.

Play the Parent vs. Kid game. This is something I found helpful when I was in school and I still do it today. When you're a parent in school, life can get so serious and stressful that it's important to have some fun. My kids are two, five, and seven, and they don't know I play this game with them. It's me versus them. They are my opponent. They are the thing fighting against me to prevent me from getting my work done. Here's the game: You give the kids something to do, start your stopwatch, then work for as fast as you can until you're interrupted. Go for as long as you can. Sometimes, it's perpetual 30-second increments and you can laugh at how ridiculously little time you have. Other times, the activity buys you lots of time and you get more done than you thought. Record the results, so you know which activities buy you more time and which don't. Anytime you can find a way to make the chaos of parenting more fun, I say go for it. It's better to laugh at the ridiculousness of the situation than to cry over the stressfulness of it.

Make sure the long-term benefits outweigh the short-term sacrifices. If you're questioning whether you should be in school, check that your math class is a stepping stone on a distinct timeline toward a distinct and worthwhile goal. It must be a necessity. Otherwise, it won't be worth the sacrifice. As I finished my Master's I considered continuing my education to get a Ph.D. in Mathematics. I liked the idea of having a Ph.D. and I liked the idea of doing more research and studying some area of Statistics in more depth, but the added benefits for tomorrow no longer outweighed the sacrifices I'd be making today. I could pursue my goal of teaching without a Ph.D. I would have added job security without a Ph.D. I would still be a strong role model without a Ph.D. That's when I stopped school, when the benefits to Future Me no longer outweighed the sacrifices I was making today.

PERMANENT PROBLEM 4: YOU WORK FULL-TIME AND ARE IN SCHOOL FULL-TIME.

As an undergraduate and graduate student, I thankfully worked for myself, tutoring students in math. It was an ideal situation, where I had high hourly rates, so I could pay the bills, and I could make my own hours, so I could schedule work around school. Balancing school with a full-time 40+ hour a week job where you must be in an office and answer to a boss is a whole other ballgame. When my husband, Joe, returned to school for a Master's in Physics, he had a full-time job as an engineer. This meant he spent forty hours a week at the office, while also attending classes at random times every day of the week. My husband is a champion and, while his initial advice to you is simply "I dunno. Just do the work," I was able to get a few more helpful pieces of advice from him. Here's a summary of Joe's advice for full-time students who work full-time:

• **Keep a strict schedule.** Know exactly when you have to be at school, clear it with your boss, and then be strict about keeping that schedule. Don't miss work for optional school events and don't miss class because you allow yourself to get roped into working.

• **Keep strict focus.** When you're at school, focus on school. When you're at work, focus on work. When you're with your family, focus on family. If you mix this up, you'll always be thinking about something else, which hinders your progress.

• **Cut back on TV and video games.** There just isn't time a lot of time when you're working and in school full-time. If you insist on watching lots of TV or playing video games, then work, school, or your relationships could suffer. All of those are more important than TV or video games.

• **Schedule breaks.** On the other side of the spectrum, don't work so hard 24/7 that you burn out. You need breaks. You need to relax and have fun. Figure out a way to schedule in some breaks that provide the rest and rejuvenation that you need.

• **Look into what benefits your company offers.** Different companies have different benefits, so it's worth looking into what your employer offers. Some allow you to cut back your hours, while still retaining your health benefits. Others will subsidize your education or allow you to take a leave of absence.

• **Get sleep.** This is obvious, but it's something Joe struggled with. He'd be up until 2 am studying, then leave for work at 4 am. It takes a toll, if you don't figure out how to make time for sleep.

• **Know when to quit.** You can only do so much and you have to prioritize. If you can't balance it all, your marriage or relationship could fall apart, you could lose your job, or you could fail out of school. If that's the case, make the choice. If your marriage is more important to you than a degree, make sure the marriage comes first. If your job is supporting and providing health care for your family, make sure it comes first. If school is your priority, don't let a relationship that's temporary anyway or a job you hate get in the way of succeeding.

• **Know why you're there.** It's a lot of work, so make sure you have a good reason to be there. Joe got his Master's in Physics, but didn't finish his Ph.D. because he didn't have a good enough reason to be there. His family came first. His job that supported our family came second. The Ph.D. was just something he wanted, but it wasn't connected to any career goals and wouldn't provide him with additional income or job security.

PERMANENT PROBLEM 5: YOU ARE AN ADULT RETURNING TO SCHOOL AFTER MANY YEARS.

If you are an adult returning to school, then you've likely forgotten a lot of the math you learned when you were in school. I waited six years before returning to school to get my Master's. Here's what I did. I acknowledged that I'd forgotten a lot of the mathematical foundations that my current classes required and I made a point to learn those foundations as I needed them. I got the books for the prerequisite classes and studied up on the stuff I'd forgotten. I asked my teacher questions and went to my school's math center. I allocated extra study time specifically to learn the things I'd forgotten. Don't try to power through without doing this. Some extra work at the beginning to brush up on things you forgot will help out a lot.

CRUSH MATH NOW

Take responsibility for your own success and brainstorm nine ways to overcome your emergency or permanent obstacle and crush math. Schedule time in a few days or a week to analyze your progress and try additional strategies.

8. WHAT TO DO IF YOU STUDY INEFFECTIVELY OR JUST DON'T UNDERSTAND MATH

Holy moly! If there's one thing I learned from all my years as a tutor, it's that some of you guys and girls are bad at studying. You can literally review your notes and homework and textbook for hours—literally *hours*—and still not be prepared for your test. If this is you, then you must know right now that reviewing your notes and homework and textbook do not count as studying. It counts as making yourself miserable and wasting your time, while you could be doing anything else in the world, including actually studying for your math test.

Here is how you study:

1. Make your best guess as to what specific questions will be on your test.
2. Learn to solve those problems *in a test-like setting*.

That's it. Here's where most students go wrong: They forget about the *in a test-like setting* part. They mistakenly think that reviewing their notes and homework and textbook are helping them learn to solve their math problems. Sure, this helps if your test is open notes, open book, in the exact same chronological order as your homework, and can be done at your leisure while at home in your pajamas. This is not how most tests are. Most tests allow no notes or books or help of any kind, so you must answer questions without the crutches you're accustomed to. Most tests are timed, so you must complete questions faster than you're accustomed to. Most tests have questions that are more jumbled and out of order, so you're solving problems that are more confusing than your nice and linearly presented notes, textbook, and homework problems.

That's right. Your homework and lessons spoon-feed the material to you, and it's your responsibility to make the jump between being spoon-fed and answering the questions on your own. Have you ever noticed how all of the problems on any given math homework assignment are similar? They're often the exact same thing, with slightly different numbers or words substituted in. If you're studying the order of operations, then all of your homework questions will be on the order of operations. If you're solving for the area and perimeter of a circle, you have a whole night's worth of homework just on that! If you're integrating trig functions, that's all you're doing for the whole evening. After you've done a couple of problems, you've figured out the pattern and can finish the rest simply by following the pattern. No more thought is required.

Then, you go to take your test, and there's no pattern. Suddenly, all of the different question types you've covered over many different homework assignments are jumbled together. There's no rhyme or reason for what goes where. There's only confusion. This is why it's common for students who otherwise "understand" everything to suddenly get confused and forget things. Of course, you're going to forget. It's a totally different scenario than what you're used to.

Therefore, reviewing your notes and figuring out how to do a test question after you've seen the pattern isn't going to help you. If anything, it is going to give you a false sense of confidence, because you haven't once looked at the questions *in a test-like setting.* Ugh, I'm getting stressed out just thinking about how inefficiently so many students study! So, let's get to it. Here are strategies to crush your inefficient study habits. I've broken down this chapter to help you crush these common challenges:

1. You don't understand the problems.
2. You can do homework but can't answer test questions.
3. You run out of time on tests.
4. You make careless errors on tests.
5. You study inefficiently the night before your test.

HOW TO STUDY IF YOU DON'T UNDERSTAND THE PROBLEMS

If you don't understand the math itself, you must experiment more with what you're doing to learn it. Don't expect to automatically, naturally be able to figure it out. Expect to have to work hard to figure it out. Expect to get confused and have to work through the confusion. Expect to get frustrated and have to work through the frustration. Expect to have to try different methods of learning. Expect there to be extra effort and time required. That's how math works.

Here are methods that I've seen help students better understand confusing math concepts:

Do the homework. Just in case you've been slacking, I have to start with this. Whether it's required or not, you must do the homework! This is the number one most crucial step to crushing math. If you haven't kept up with the homework, stop reading this book right now and go do your math home-work. Once you've caught up on all of your homework, and I mean every single question in every single assignment, then come back and read the book. Until then, the only thing that will help you understand the problems better, the only thing that will help you do better on your exams, the only thing that will ultimately raise your grade, is to complete the homework. Thoroughly. So get to it.

Have someone explain it to you. If you take math long enough, you'll eventually hit a point where you can't figure it out on your own. It happened to me. It happened to Harper and Priscilla and Dylan. And perhaps it's happened to you, too. If that's the case, the solution is simple: You need to ask for help. Ask your teacher. Ask a parent. Ask a friend. Go to the math center. Hire a tutor. Find somebody who will help you figure it out. If you're reluctant to do this and would rather waste hours upon hours upon hours simply for the sake of doing it alone, read Chapter 6. Maybe that can knock some sense into you.

Explain it to someone else. The best way to learn some-thing is to teach it to somebody else. Find a friend, classmate, brother, sister, or parent, and explain the steps to them. Go to the math center and instead of asking them for help, explain the steps to them and get feedback. Knowing a problem well enough to explain it to someone else adds a layer of depth to your understanding. This is why the best tutors don't explain the material to you but instead ask you how to do it, have you explain and give you feedback.

Find alternate resources. High school and college-level math is not rocket science. There's nothing new under the sun, and there are millions of resources available to help you learn the material. If your textbook isn't working for you, find one that does. If you learn better through videos, go to Khan

Academy or YouTube. Watching a good video is like getting a new teacher or tutor for free! If you like textbooks but have a terrible one, take a trip to the library to find an author who can explain the math in a way that makes sense. I know you probably think that all math textbooks are tedious, boring, painful, and awful, but the truth is that some are better at explaining things than others. Find the one that works for you, and use it as a resource to help you understand the problems better.

HOW TO STUDY IF YOU CAN DO HOMEWORK BUT CAN'T ANSWER TEST QUESTIONS

If you can do all your homework but can't answer test questions, you must focus on the *in a test-like setting* part of studying. This is simple. Do the following:

1. Make a list of potential test questions. Maybe your teacher gave this to you in the review, or maybe you have to guess. Don't worry about this being perfect. If you're guessing, think about which questions (1) came up most in the homework and (2) were emphasized the most in class. Start with these questions first. Err on the side of including harder questions, rather than easier ones.

2. Create a practice quiz. Pick random questions from the list and write them all out on paper.

3. Set the timer. Yes, time yourself. Make it a short period of time (slightly less than you think you can answer the questions in) or slightly less time than you'll have per question on the real test.

4. Take the quiz. If you're stressed out here, good. If you blank out here, good. If you can't answer a question here, good. You want to get all of the bad tests out of the way during your practice quizzes. You want to make all of your mistakes now, so you can learn from your mistakes and not make them on the actual test. Speaking of which...

5. Learn from your mistakes. Did you miss any questions? Go back and redo those problems. Figure out exactly what you did wrong. Was there one thing or multiple things you missed? Did you forget a formula or get jumbled in the middle of a long calculation? Put this question on your Don't Know list. (Remember, this is the list of things that you need to come back to and study.) Lastly, write down how you can remember to do this correctly on the test.

6. Repeat. Once you've reviewed your practice quiz, take another quiz but with different questions. Learn from your mistakes again. Repeat as many times as you need. If you get 100% on your practice quiz, make a quiz with harder questions. Use your judgment and repeat until you know everything you need to know *in a test-like setting*. If you're taking a quiz, you may only need to do this once. If you're taking a cumulative final exam, you may need to do this many times.

7. Study your Don't Know list. You missed these questions on your practice test. You reviewed them and made some notes after each practice test. Review them again. Make a list of common errors. Is there a formula you forgot multiple times? Is there a careless error that you made multiple times? Anything that comes up more than once, take note of it. These are the mistakes you are the most likely to make and, if you can pinpoint them now, you can avoid them on the actual test.

That's it. For other problems, there are many different solutions that I found to work for students. Something that might work for one student may not work for another student. But in this particular case, there is actually one universal solution. Follow the above steps, which I followed with hundreds of students, and you will be wildly more prepared for your math test than you have been in the past.

CRUSH MATH NOW

Create a practice test. Pick random homework problems that you think might be on your next test. Write them down on a piece of paper. Set the timer and take your quiz. Correct it and review your mistakes. Done! You just tried a powerful new study strategy!

HOW TO STUDY IF YOU BLANK OUT ON FORMULAS

If you're one of the students who blanks out on math formulas during exams, there are two strategies that work here:

1. Understand the formulas.
2. Memorize the formulas.

You need to utilize both techniques in order to crush math. Let's take a closer look at when you need each.

Understand a Simple Example of the Formula. For example, if you're trying to remember the slope intercept formula, $y = mx+b$, it might be easier to remember $y = 2x+1$ instead. You start a one on the y-axis (because the y-intercept is one), then go up two and over one (because the slope is two). Then you can take that pattern and apply it to other problems. Since in this example you know what to do when you have a positive slope and y-intercept, you can deduct what you would do if you had negative numbers instead. Sometimes understanding an example is easier than memorizing the formula.

Understand the Formulas. In other scenarios, it makes sense to understand the formula itself. Take whatever part of the formula you can't remember and figure out why it's there. If you can't remember the point-slope form of a linear equation, try to figure out why it has an x_1 and y_1, while the slope-intercept form doesn't. If you're confused about p-values and the Student's t distribution, figure out how it's similar to and different from the Normal Distribution that you've spent so much time learning. If you can't remember the Black-Scholes equation, it's because this isn't a partial differential equation you're supposed to just memorize. Understanding how it's derived is essential to using it. Students often try to buckle down and memorize these things, instead of understanding them. What I'm telling you is that in some cases it actually *saves you time* and *raises your grade* to understand them.

Understand and Use Both. Sometimes you need both of these tools to succeed. If you are learning the point-slope form for a linear equation, finding p-values in Statistics, or using the Black-Scholes equation, it might be helpful to both (1) understand the formula and (2) understand a simple example of the formula. The more a formula confuses you, the more important it is to utilize both of these strategies.

Other times, you just need to buckle down and do the memorization. For this, I want you to take a moment and think about how you prepare for classes that are very heavy on memorization. Have you taken Spanish 1 or history or biology? If so, what did you do when you had to memorize new Spanish words or historical dates or a bazillion new biology terms? Math is just like any other subject. Sometimes, you just have to buckle down and memorize. Do what works for other classes. If you do well in Spanish or history or biology, then memorize your math formula using the same techniques. If you're also struggling to remember dates, formulas, and vocabulary in other classes, then the following memorization techniques will help you for both math and your other memorization-heavy classes:

Make flashcards. I don't know why math students don't think to do this. Students who struggle in math mistakenly think that "math people" are able to just "automatically" or "naturally" remember math formulas. Math people cannot do this. They just make flashcards when they need to.

Write the formulas down repeatedly. Personally, I hate flashcards. I'm just not a visual or auditory learner. I hear something, and it's in one ear, out the other. I see something, and I forget it the minute I look away. I have to write things down in order to remember them. Therefore, if you're like me, writing down the formulas might be more helpful than using flashcards. Make a list of all the formulas you need to learn. On a piece of paper, write down every formula you can remember. Track the ones you can't remember. Those are the ones you need to quiz yourself on again the following day. It's basically using flashcards but instead of saying the formula or thinking it in your head, you're writing it down.

Find another way to quiz yourself. The key to memorizing formulas is to quiz yourself, rather than passively read over formulas. If flashcards don't work for you and writing the formulas down repeatedly doesn't work for you, then find another way that works. Have a friend or parent quiz you on the formulas. Make digital flashcards. It doesn't matter how you quiz yourself. What matters is that you take responsibility for your own success and find a way that works for you.

The last crucial part of understanding and memorizing formulas has to do with *when* you are trying to accomplish this. *When* you memorize formulas is just as important as what you do to memorize them.

Don't try to memorize all your formulas the night before your test. The problem with cramming all your memorization is that your work gets multiplied by three. If it would normally take you one hour divvied up throughout the week to commit the formulas to memory, it will take you three hours the night before the test. If you would have to write down a formula 10 times divvied up throughout the week to commit the formulas to memory, you'll have to write it down 30 times the night before the test. If you have to study a flashcard 100 times throughout the week to memorize a formula, you'll have to study it 300 times the night before the test.

Trying to memorize formulas the night before the test is not just inefficient studying, it's a legitimate studying error. Why? Because if you need three hours to memorize all the formulas, you don't make it to the full three hours that you need. If you have to study a flashcard 30 times the night before the test, you burn out at 25. It's not just that memorizing formulas throughout the week saves you time, it's that saving all your memorization for the night before the test guarantees that you won't spend a sufficient amount of time memorizing your formulas. It guarantees that you'll blank out during a test and chalk it up to not being a math person, instead of recognizing that you failed to memorize throughout the week.

Memorizing a formula takes anywhere from thirty seconds to five minutes per day, if you spread your memorization out over the week, so make that your go-to memorization strategy. Review flashcards *throughout the week*. Write down the formulas *throughout the week*. Memorize somehow *throughout the week*. Remember *throughout the week*, and you'll crush those formulas on your next test.

HOW TO STUDY IF YOU MAKE CARELESS ERRORS

Everybody chalks little mistakes up to careless errors. It's a way of letting yourself off the hook while also blaming nothing. It absolves you from having to fix the problem. I'm going to be honest here: If you make careless errors on exams—particularly if you make mistakes on things you know how to do on the longer or harder problems—these mistakes are not careless. Careless errors stem from one of two things:

(1) not knowing the current material well enough or

(2) gaps in your foundations that need to be fixed.

Right now, I know you're thinking something like, "Baloney!! I wrote down $-2 \times 3 = 6$ on my last test. Obviously, I know that $-2 \times 3 = -6$. It is so basic! *That* is not a gap in my foundations. It was a 'careless error.'" Here's the thing: That was most likely a small step in a more complex problem. If you don't know that longer, more complex problem well enough, your brain gets overloaded, and, yeah, you make "careless errors" like that. The problem isn't that you don't know $-2 \times 3 = -6$. The problem is that you don't know the longer, more complex problem well enough. If this is the case, you need to study those harder, longer, more complex problems...well... more. You need to know them better. You need to be able to work through them faster and more confidently. You need to be able to solve them quickly and efficiently *in a test-like setting* prior to your test. When you can do this, the careless errors miraculously disappear.

On the other hand, this mistake could be from the fact that you do, in fact, have gaps in your foundations, meaning there's math from last semester or even four years ago that you ought to know but don't actually know well enough. The mistake "$-2 \times 3 = 6$" is actually a common one, because many students don't know their rules for negative numbers well enough. They know the rules enough to acknowledge the errors when they see them, but they don't know the rules well enough to automatically get those steps correct in a larger problem. It's like passively reviewing your textbook. Just as it's easy to say, "Oh, I understand that," when looking at a problem in the textbook, it's easy to say, "Oh, I understand that," when looking at a mistake a teacher circled with a red pen on your test. Knowing something in retrospect or knowing something when you're reviewing it is a lower level of understanding than knowing it *in a test-like setting*. Stop blaming careless errors and work on better understanding the material, whether it's current problems or gaps in foundations.

How do you do this? Look at your mistakes. If you tend to make lots of mistakes with positive and negative signs, go back and learn those rules. Don't go back and re-read the rules. We've established that's a waste of time. Do practice problems with positive and negative signs. Do deliberate, repeated practice on those foundations that you're lacking. Do deliberate, repeated practice on those complex problems where you make mistakes.

CRUSH MATH NOW

Look over your old tests and quizzes. In your *Crush Math Now Game Plan*, add questions you answered incorrectly or errors you made to your *Don't Know It* list.

9. WHAT TO DO IF YOU STUDY AND TAKE TESTS TOO SLOWLY

If you feel like you study too slowly, and therefore don't finish homework and tests, it's likely for one of the following reasons:

You're bad at estimating how long things take. It's okay. This is a skill set that can be learned just like any other skill set. As a student, it's an important one to master sooner rather than later.

You lose focus easily. No judgment. The whole world may be more interesting than your math homework, so yeah, you're distracted by everything under the sun.

You do everything. If your teacher says to read the textbook, you diligently read and highlight it. If your teacher says to watch a video, you do that, too. If she tells you to show all your work on the homework, you take the extra time to make it neat. Whatever is asked of you, you do it without cutting corners.

You get stuck on the hardest questions. Easy and medium questions follow a normal pace, but those hard questions—the ones at the end of an assignment—can trip you up for hours. They can turn a 25-minute assignment into a frustrating 90 minutes of your life, wasted.

You're over-scheduled. Whether you're working, juggling extracurriculars, or taking a large course load, the bottom line is you don't have time. You're too busy to spend a normal amount of time on homework or studying math and, therefore, need to be able to expedite the time it takes.

You're just slow. Some students are just slow at math. You feel like being slow at finishing math is just part of who you are as opposed to some obstacle that needs to be overcome. If that's you, you need to squash that thinking right now. Even if you have a medically confirmed learning disability that qualifies you for extra time on your exams, you can still take measures to expedite how long your homework and studying take. Don't make excuses. Whatever your situation is, you can improve.

First, however, I want to introduce you to the classic time management technique called the Pomodoro Technique. It's used by engineering teams at Google, as well as anywhere else you find crazy-productive people. It is an effective tool, regardless of the reason *why* you feel you study too slowly.

THE POMODORO TECHNIQUE

Once upon a time, there was a college student named Francesco Cirillo who just couldn't bring himself to read his sociology book. He had an exam coming up and needed to focus, but his mind kept wandering. There was just so much reading and work to do and his mind kept wandering to other things. Then he had a realization. Instead of focusing on the big picture, the monumental task of reading the whole book and studying for his exam, he decided to focus on *now*. He set his timer and read for ten minutes.

When the timer went off, he realized he'd actually focused. He'd actually read and made progress. In just ten minutes, he'd regained control of his studying. He could now break this momentous task of reading his sociology book into bite-size chunks of time. Over the years, he experimented with this method and eventually it evolved into the well-known time-management method called The Pomodoro Technique.

Here's a simplified version of the Pomodoro Technique, which takes exactly 30 minutes and, in it's simplest form, requires only two steps:

1. Write down what you'll work on.
2. Set a timer for 25 minutes and work on just that.
3. Take a five-minute break, then repeat.

That's it. It's so simple, it's, quite frankly, brilliant.

The idea behind it, which you can learn more about in *The Pomodoro Technique* by Francesco Cirillo, is that 5 minutes is too short to accomplish much and 60 minutes is too long to concentrate, so you build your workday (or, in your case, your study sessions) around 25-minute sprints. Instead of always forcing yourself to keep going until you get interrupted or too distracted or too frustrated with math, you end at 25 minutes.

Mentally speaking, it's important to not end your math sessions in frustration. When you practice soccer, you practice for a set period of time, and then stop. You don't go until you're exhausted and frustrated and hating soccer. If you did that, everyone would hate soccer. When you practice piano, you practice for a set period of time, and then stop. You don't play until your hands cramp up and you want to punch the piano. If everyone did that, everyone would hate playing the piano. Likewise, when you study math, you must study for a set period of time, and then stop. You don't study until you're exhausted, frustrated, and hating math.

The Pomodoro Technique helps you study math the way you practice soccer, piano, or anything else. In particular, it offers these benefits:

Pomodoros help you estimate how long things take. When you write down what you will work on, you're making an estimate of how much work you can do in 25 minutes. When your timer goes off, you see how much you actually got done. By constantly doing this, you'll become better at judging how long assignments and studying take.

Pomodoros help you focus. If you don't know how long you'll study, it's easy to get distracted by anything and everything. If you know you're only studying for 25 minutes, you can power through, stay focused, and get more done in a shorter period of time.

Pomodoros teach you to study faster. Think of how you work during tests, when the timer is running and you know you must finish within a set period of time. You work faster and harder. You get through more problems in one test than in several homework sessions. This is because it's timed. You'll have the same amount of work, but if you can do it twice as quickly, you'll spend half as much time on it.

Pomodoros help you create habits. If you have 25 minutes of math and you're done, then this is a doable amount of studying. It's not too stressful to get started. It's easier to just do it. And that's what you want when creating a habit: something that's doable. If you say you want to study math for two hours every night, then you're setting yourself up for failure because, seriously, who is actually going to follow through with that?

The second step in the Pomodoro Technique is taking a break, and it's equally important. After your Pomodoro is done, give yourself a 5-minute break. Get up and walk around. Relax. Give your mind a rest, and don't think about math. This offers several benefits:

Pomodoros help manage distractions. By giving yourself five minutes to check your phone notifications during your break, it'll be easier to ignore them during your Pomodoro (during which your phone should be silenced). Check your text messages, Instagram updates, or any other phone notifications during your break, *not* during your Pomodoro.

Pomodoros allow ideas to percolate. Math problems can get confusing and frustrating. Often, it's hard to see the answer when you're in the moment, and it's better to come back to it later. Often, the five-minute breaks you get are all you need for inspiration to hit you. You might remember a formula you forgot, recall a problem from class that was similar, or just find that skimming through the chapter might give you clues.

Pomodoros help you manage stress. Thinking about everything else you have to do, while simultaneously doing math, makes math stressful. Spending lots of time on math, when there are so many other things you need to do, makes math stressful. By cutting the distractions and studying faster, the Pomodoro Technique can help make math less stressful.

That's it. The Pomodoro Technique is 25 minutes of focused study followed by a 5-minute break. You can repeat it as many times as you need, so if you're working on an assignment that can't be completed in 25 minutes, simply repeat. Set the timer and study for another 25 minutes.

CRUSH MATH NOW

Get out your math homework, set your timer for 25 minutes, and go! Do your first math Pomodoro.

Now let's move on to the specific challenges that are slowing you down.

PROBLEM 1: YOU LOSE FOCUS EASILY

One of the problems with studying math is that you might consider *everything* in the world to be more interesting than math, so you're constantly distracted from studying it. The downside to this is that the more you are distracted, the longer you end up studying math. So, often, students "study" math for thirty minutes but only get five minutes' worth of work done because they're distracted the whole time...so they have to study more and more, again and again. It's a vicious cycle. The Pomodoro Technique will help you with this, but if you lose focus easily, a simple timer may not be enough. You'll need to take extra precautions to help you focus.

Here are some suggestions that have helped me and my students create a workspace that enables you to focus so that you can work more productively and get work done faster.

Lose the phone. If you're studying math, turn your phone off. At the very least, silence the notifications. No email. No texting. No social media. If you can't figure out how to turn off your notifications (yes, I've heard this excuse before), I challenge you to figure out how. Most smartphones have a "Do Not Disturb" function that will silence any notification alerts but still allow them to appear on your screen, so you can check them on your break time. If you don't know how to activate that function, a quick Google search of "How to turn on Do Not Disturb for —your phone model—" can clear things up. Become the kind of person who won't let mini obstacles like distracting phone notifications prevent you from crushing math.

Isolate yourself from the world. If your friends will freak out when they can't reach you immediately (yes, I've heard this excuse too), then give your friends a heads up that you're turning off your notifications for twenty-five minutes. Overcome the obstacle.

Lose the visual distractions. Now that people and your phone won't distract you, let's deal with visual distractions. Yes, I know students who will literally stare at a photo on the wall instead of doing math. If that's you, then lose the picture of your boyfriend on your desk. Move the pile of bills you need to pay. Put away the book you need to read for another class. Out of sight, out of mind. If you like simplicity, go for blank walls and a clear desk. If you like motivational stuff, put up inspiring quotes. Above my desk is the quote, "Your Goals Don't Care How You Feel." It reminds me to get back to work every time my mind starts to wander. It makes me work a little faster and a little harder, every time I look up and see it.

Lose the music with lyrics. Your favorite music may get you energized, but it may very much distract you from math. It's hard to focus on complicated subjects when song lyrics are competing for your attention. Here are your options for noise while studying:

- Silence
- Rain/ocean/nature sounds
- Vacuum cleaner sounds

- Classical
- Eletronica with no lyrics

Extra tip: Make sure your playlist is at least twenty-five minutes long, so you're not distracted by changing songs during your Pomodoro.

Last but not least, you may lack focus because you're stressed, angry, sad, or feeling any other emotion that hinders problem-solving. There's nothing worse than trying to solve math problems, when you're already super frustrated. In this case, the best thing you can do is deal with your source of stress, anger, or sadness before jumping into your math homework.

Make a list of the problems that are stressing you out, angering you, or making you sad. Sometimes just getting it out of your head and onto paper is enough to improve your mood and focus. If that's not enough to get you in the right mindset for tackling math, make a list of solutions to your stress-inducing problems.

Do something that relaxes you before you start your math homework. Read an uplifting book. Do a quick meditation. Make a quick phone call to that friend who always makes you feel better. Whatever you do, taking a few minutes to acknowledge and deal with your source of stress, anger, or sadness will help you focus on math and get through it faster.

PROBLEM 2: YOU DO EVERYTHING

You're a good, dependable, studious student. And you're reading this whole book, right? Even though I told you just to read the first two chapters and then jump to the one or two chapters that will help you the most, you're reading the whole book. That's your problem right there. You do everything, instead of figuring out the one or two things that will have the most impact. Nobody is correcting you because you're trying, and that's all that teachers and parents really want: a student who tries.

But you are not your teacher or your parent. You have bigger goals for yourself than "being a student who tries." Therefore, you must hold yourself to a higher standard. You must figure out how to succeed without doing everything, and you do this with the 80/20 rule, also known as The Pareto Principle.

The 80/20 rule says that if you try many different things— because this principle pertains to big numbers—80 percent of your results will come from 20 percent of the things you do. In other words, if you focus on the changes, strategies, and questions that will have the largest impact on your math grade, you can do less while achieving more.

I want you to understand how powerful this rule is, let's first talk about how the 80/20 rule plays out in life. Twenty percent of life's activities get you 80 percent of what you want in life. For example, twenty percent of your time spent yields 80 percent of the results you want. Eighty percent of reducing your stress will come from cutting or fixing 20 percent of the stressful things in your life. Eighty percent of your happiness comes from 20 percent of the things you do or 20 percent of the people you spend time with. In a nutshell, 80 percent of everything awesome comes from finding the 20 percent of things that create awesomeness.

What exactly does this mean for math? It means that if you're wasting time doing things that have little to no effect on your math grade, you're losing time for the things that matter the most. Here are the specifics of the 80/20 Rule:

Crushing math: Eighty percent of your improvement in math will come from 20 percent of the things you do. If you're not getting the grade you want in math, try different things to see which 20 percent will provide 80 percent of the impact on your grade. *You don't need to do more. You need to find the things that work.*

Time: Eighty percent of your improvement in math will come from 20 percent of the time you spend studying math. If you spend hours studying and are *not* getting the grades you want, you're not spending your time on the right things. *You do not need to study more. You need to study differently.*

Motivation: Of the many reasons you should be motivated to crush math, 80 percent of your motivation to succeed in math will come from only 20 percent of those reasons. If you lack the motivation to do the things you know you should do, you have not found a strong enough reason why. *You do not need more reasons to be motivated. You just need a few reasons that are very powerful.*

People: Twenty percent of the people who can help you with math will provide 80 percent of the help. If you've reached out to friends, teachers, or tutors and have not found anyone helpful, you've likely not reached out enough to find the people who will help you the most. *You shouldn't give up on asking for help and try to figure out how to do this alone. You need to study with different people.*

Textbook: Eighty percent of what you need to know comes from 20 percent of your textbook. Please do not read your textbook cover to cover. Most of it will be redundant with your class notes and homework. Skim through it. Check out the summary at the end of each section or chapter. Read only specific formulas or examples that you need. *You don't need to read every word. You just need to find the few details that will help you.*

Change: Eighty percent of your improvement in math will come from 20 percent of the changes that you make as a result of this book. Which 20 percent ends up impacting your grade the most is determined by who you are: your personality, your life, your class, your unique situation, etc. You must actively work to customize your math study routine. If you don't, 80 percent of your time could be wasted. *You don't need to read this whole book. You need to focus on the chapter or two that will have the biggest impact on your grade.*

In addition to looking for the 20 percent of things that will have the most impact on your grade, I also want you to really understand how much time you have. There are exactly 420 minutes between 3 and 10 pm. You should take one hour for dinner and visiting with family or friends. That brings you to 360 minutes. If you play sports or do another kind of extracurricular activity, that's another 120 minutes subtracted. That brings you down to 240 minutes. The last 60 minutes should be reserved for things you can do when you're exhausted. The easy stuff. The no-mental-exertion-required tasks. Easier homework assignments that are just busy work, for instance, or required reading, which happens a lot for English and history. Those will take up your last 60 minutes. That leaves you with roughly 180 minutes, or three hours, before you hit mental exhaustion. If you're struggling to get it all done, it's because, when you actually look at it, most of your hard work must be done in a 3-hour window. Plan accordingly. You cannot do everything. You must find the 20 percent of things that matter, and do those.

CRUSH MATH NOW

Make a list of everything you did to study for your last math test. Rank it from most helpful to least helpful. Do more of the most helpful things. Cut anything that's just wasting your time. Swap them out for something new. Try something different and see if it has more impact.

PROBLEM 3: HARD QUESTIONS TAKE FOREVER

You do well on most of the homework, but those last few questions take forever. They're harder than the rest. They're harder than the class examples. They might not match up with any examples in the book or your notes. There's always something you're missing. They take you forever, and you're scared that they might be on your next test. If you're a B student trying to pull up to an A, these are the questions that could single-handedly prevent you from reaching your goal. The following are my suggestions.

Look for patterns. Even the hardest questions are related to what you've been studying in class. First, find how the question relates to the things you've been studying. There's almost always a pattern or some similar starting point. Then, look at how the question differs from those you've already solved.

Look for missing information. It's possible that you just missed something that the teacher or textbook covered, so you're trying to solve the problem with incomplete information or an incomplete skill set. Read back through your notes for anything you might have missed. Read through your textbook for anything you might have missed. If you've picked up alternate textbooks, look through those also. Sometimes, when an alternate textbook explains things in a slightly different way, it's easier to see the pattern.

Go to your teacher's office hours. One of my A students came to office hours during finals week. She'd never needed to come to office hours before because she usually breezed through the homework, but as soon as she hit three problems she couldn't do, during a week that was packed with other finals and papers, she immediately asked for help. There are times when it's appropriate to "power through" and figure it out yourself. I'm all for that. But there are also times when you need to save some time and asking for help is the quickest way to accomplish that. Students who crush math don't hesitate to ask for help when it's in their best interest.

Make time by studying easy and medium questions faster. You should have different goals when you study different question types. On a test, if you take too long on easy and medium questions, then you're not leaving yourself enough time at the end of the test to answer the hard questions. Therefore, when you study easy and medium questions, your goal is to do them as quickly and correctly as possible. Sprint through them to make more time for the harder questions.

Settle for good enough. Ever notice how apps are always updating? That's because they make the app good enough and send it out to the world, knowing that they can fix it later on. Same goes for math. You don't have to do 100 percent of your homework on time 100 percent of the time. Sometimes it's more efficient to settle for good enough. Ask the teacher in class how to do the hard question that was holding you up. Your teacher will be thrilled you asked a question, and, if you're struggling with it, odds are you have classmates who are too, so you just helped them out as well.

CRUSH MATH NOW

On your next homework assignment, circle the hardest questions. Estimate how much time they will take and build extra time into your schedule to figure them out.

PROBLEM 4: YOU'RE OVER-SCHEDULED

You're over-scheduled, so you don't have time to read a paragraph describing being over-scheduled. Let's just get to the helpful strategies for over-scheduled students:

Use class time to do homework. Every semester, there's a class where the teacher wastes a lot of time. How can you use this to your advantage? Get your math work done during class. Study during class. Sprint through the easy questions. Try the hard questions, ponder, come back, and try again. Create a list of potential test questions you need to quiz yourself on later. The best times to get through work in classes that waste your time is (1) during attendance or other time-consuming, beginning-of-class stuff, (2) when that one student who asks long, irrelevant questions that don't pertain to anyone else is talking, and (3) whenever else there is wasted time. You're there anyway. Use the time to your advantage. This worked wonders for me when I had an Algebra II class that wasted *so* much time, I completed nearly 100 percent of my math homework in the class itself.

Just say no. If you tend to be overscheduled, it's because, like me, you tend to automatically say yes instead of no. While the "yes" philosophy to life is a positive, uplifting, motivating, go-get-'em mentality, it can, when out of control, overwhelm you and spread you too thin, so you're not making progress on anything. Unfortunately, no matter how much you want to do everything, every opportunity you say yes to means you're automatically saying no to something else. More specifically, if you're too busy for math, then everything you say yes to means saying no to crushing math. If math is important to your long-term goals, you need to reassess the other things you're saying yes to. If the other things are not in line with your goals, like crushing math is, then just say no.

Embrace batching. Batching is getting one type of work (i.e., math) done all at the same time. For example, instead of working a little every night on math, consider getting all your math homework done for the week on one day, dedicating another day entirely to another class and so on. Sometimes spreading out the work is more efficient, but sometimes batching is more efficient. Here's how I would schedule my days using batching during soccer season in high school.

- **Sunday would be my math day.** Because I knew my math assignments ahead of time, I would get through as much math as I could for the week on Sunday. I would do all the homework and even prep for Friday's test. Then, there'd be minimal work left for the week—just a quick review on Thursday night.
- **Monday would be my paper-writing day.** I'd get the topics for my two weekly AP English papers on Monday, so I couldn't start them over the weekend. I'd write rough drafts of both papers on Monday, plus do all of Monday's homework. Plus do as much of Tuesday's homework as I could.
- **Tuesday would be my soccer day.** I would do minimal homework, whatever was due Wednesday and didn't get done before.
- **Wednesday would be my homework day.** I'd try to complete everything due Thursday and Friday. Draft two of both English papers and review for my math test.
- **Thursday would be another soccer day.** It's not

to say that I wouldn't do school work on Thursday; there'd always be some left over, such as a last-minute review for the test and the final draft of two papers. It'd still be a late night, but it was doable. If I'd saved all my math studying and writing of both papers from scratch until the night before, I'd likely be grounded the next week and not allowed to play soccer.

- **Friday is my fun day.** Finally, time to relax. If your schedule is so crazy that you must plan ahead like this, make sure you schedule in a fun day at the end of it all.

Get the important stuff done early. Some of the most successful people in the world wake up earlier than everyone else to get the most important things done first...before the rest of the world starts distracting them. In high school, my life wasn't so crazy that I needed to resort to this. However, during my Master's program, when I was juggling a newborn baby, working and school, I absolutely did. Likewise, as I write this book—and juggle teaching math, raising three kids under the age of ten, and coaching their soccer teams—yeah, life is once again so crazy that I wake up at the crack of dawn to get the book done, because it's important to me. If you hate mornings but your life has reached a level of crazy that requires waking up at 5 am to do your math homework, then read *The Miracle Morning for College Students* by Hal Elrod and Natalie Janji to help you do what you need to do. Take responsibility for your success, and get the important stuff done early.

CRUSH MATH NOW

Make a list of all your obligations, everything that takes up time, and say no to as many things as possible. Cancel them until math is crushed. Postpone them until math is crushed. Neglect them until math is crushed. Put your most important goals first. Crush math first.

10. WHAT TO DO IF YOU'RE FAILING OR DOING POORLY ON TESTS

Most of the preparation for your next test has been covered in other chapters because most of your preparation comes *before* the night before your test. If you struggle with any of the following problems, go back and read the corresponding chapter to help you fix the problem *before* the night before your test. If you blank out, freeze or have panic attacks on your tests, then read Chapter 2 and crush your lack of confidence. If you make careless errors or simply don't understand the material well enough to do well on your math test, then read Chapters 6 and 8 to figure out how to get the help you need and learn the material. If you run out of time on your math tests, read Chapter 9 and figure out how to improve your pacing, while simultaneously doing your homework.

All of these things must be tackled *before* the night before your test. This chapter will walk you through what to do the actual night before your test, the few minutes right before your test starts, and during your test. While there are certainly more specific strategies and hacks that pertain to specific math classes, this chapter focuses on test-taking strategies that can give students in any math class an extra edge on their math tests. The beauty of it is that many of these strategies will help you in your other classes as well.

HOW TO STUDY THE NIGHT BEFORE YOUR MATH TEST

Before we talk about what to do the night before your math test, let's talk about what you *don't* do the night before other important events. A marathon runner does not learn how to run the night before the marathon. They have already learned how to do this. They are also not at home Googling "how long is a marathon." An Olympic swimmer doesn't learn how to swim the night before the Olympics. They are also not at home Googling "tips on swimming better" and getting stressed out. A piano player doesn't sit down for the first time to practice their piece the night before their recital...unless they want to embarrass themselves at the recital. These are not strategies for success! You must understand that being prepared *before* the night before your exam is the best strategy for success.

Here are some tips for studying *before* the night before your test:

Do 100 percent of your homework. Homework is not optional. If your teacher says it is optional, this is because they simply don't have time to grade it, not because you don't need to complete it. Make time for homework. Crush those excuses. Commit to it. Figure out a time and place, and get it done. Homework is not an unrealistic recommendation that no one is expected to keep up with. Homework is the bare minimum. Additionally, homework shouldn't take you long. If it does, read Chapter 9 and focus on your efficiency until it takes less time to finish. Life is too short to spend it all on math homework, but math homework is too important to skip.

Learn from your mistakes. When students are bad at

studying, learning from mistakes is the thing they miss. They try. Their hearts are in the right place, but, if they forget to learn from mistakes, they can study too much without really doing anything to better their grade. You must look at the mistakes you made on homework, quizzes, and tests and figure out where you went wrong so you never make the same mistake again. You must experiment with different ways of studying and *analyze* what you did, what worked and what didn't. You must learn from mistakes.

Use the Pomodoro Technique. Across the board, students I meet study too much! They go too slowly, get distracted, get overwhelmed, and end up giving up or spending more time than they should on math. Focus, so you can succeed in as little time as possible. The Pomodoro Technique will help you with that. (More on that in Chapter 9 also.)

That was my advice for *before* the night before your test. Now, here's my advice for the night before your test:

Study however and whatever will help you the most.

That's it.

You're probably thinking, "*What*!?" That's right. Study however and whatever will help you the most. There is no one-size-fits-all formula for studying the night before the exam. Between my four high school math classes, ten undergrad math classes, and sixteen Master's math classes, I've learned one thing: Every test is different. Sometimes I'm already prepared the night before the test; other times, I'm not. Sometimes the material is easy; other times, it's crazy hard. Sometimes I know what'll be on the test; other times, I haven't a clue. Sometimes I have lots of time to study; other times, I have none. Sometimes I am focused on math; other times, all the craziness in the world is pulling my attention in different directions.

The point is that how prepared you are, how much time you have, and what you know about the test varies from class to class, teacher to teacher, and even test to test. So, successful math students recognize that they must take responsibility for their own success and do what's best for them in their exact situation. That being said, here are three levels of preparedness you'll find yourself in:

1. You're totally not prepared.
2. You're kinda prepared.
3. You're mostly prepared.

If you're mostly prepared or kinda prepared, you can do the easy and medium questions, no problem, but are still nervous about the hard questions. Do a quick review of the things you know, then focus your time learning from your mistakes and solving hard questions *in a test-like setting*. What mistakes did you make on homework and quizzes? What mistakes might you make on your test, and how can you remember to not make those mistakes on the test? Then, look for curveballs, any hard questions that the teacher will put on the test to differentiate between students who get an A and students who get a B. What hard questions are most likely to be on the test? What hard questions are you afraid will be on the test? If it scares you, that's what you need to study.

The rest of my advice for students who are *mostly* and *kinda* prepared is similar to those who are *totally not* prepared, so read on, but recognize that your situation isn't this dire and just take what you need from it.

WHAT TO DO IF YOU'RE TOTALLY UNPREPARED

If your test is tomorrow and you're totally unprepared, don't freak out. You can totally do this, but before we get into how you'll do this, let's talk about what you should absolutely **not** do:

- Read this entire book.
- Waste your energy fighting with mom and dad.
- Complain about math or your teacher on social media.
- Wallow in regret for not having studied more already.
- Google jobs that don't require math.
- Google majors that don't require math.
- Ask why life is so unfair.
- Ask why you're not smart.
- Ask why math is so hard.
- Give up and watch TV.
- Cry.

Why? Because you want to be the kind of person who succeeds in life. You want to be a warrior and a champion. You want to be crazy rich, crazy happy, and crazy awesome. You want to be so awesome that, at the end of it all, you can look back at your life and say, "If I had to do it over again, I'd do it exactly the same." The kind of person you want to be is *not* the kind of person who gives up the night before a stupid little math test.

What you are going to do, if you're unprepared the night before your test, is go all in. Make the commitment to give math 100 percent of your focus and energy for one night, and do everything you can to pass the test. To do this, I want to share with you three secrets that A math students know. And it's not just A math students who understand this. Navy Seals, Olympians, and billionaires also understand this. Here are the three secrets you must understand:

1. You cannot change what you did yesterday and every day before.
2. You cannot control what you will face tomorrow.
3. You can *only* control what you do *today*.

And when the stakes are high, you go all in *today*. You give it your best *today*. You work as crazy hard as you can *today*. You do everything in your power *today* to get the results you want. So make *today* the day you will fight for your math grade. Fight like your life depends on it.

Pretend math is a bear, and you're stuck in a cage with it.

It's probably going to eat you alive, but you fight like a champion anyway. You might get "lucky" and succeed. You might get what you deserve (from not studying enough) and fail. Regardless of the outcome, you'll be able to look in the mirror and say, "*Today*, I gave it everything I had. *Today*, I have no regrets. If I had to do *today* over again, I'd do it exactly the same."

The following is a study plan I use with my students help them make the most of today. It alternates what you're studying every thirty minutes so that you're forced to focus on what's important instead of getting distracted, only studying one topic, and not getting to the rest. I call this study plan the Alternating Pomodoro. If you didn't read about The Pomodoro Technique in Chapter 9, here's all you need to know: Each Pomodoro is a half hour long and consists of 25 minutes of intense studying, followed by a five-minute break.

THE ALTERNATING POMODORO

Pomodoro 1: Review and create three lists of questions to study.

1. Review your notes, homework, and study guide, if you have one. Memorize formulas, theorems, vocabulary, etc. Read through the *summaries* for each chapter in your book.
2. As you review, make three practice lists: easy questions, medium questions, hard questions. When possible, choose questions with answers so you can check your work.
3. Do not read entire chapters. Do not put every homework question on your practice lists. Force yourself to guess at what questions are most likely to be on the test.

Pomodoro 2: Tackle as many medium questions as you can.

1. Don't stress if they're miscategorized. Some may be easy; some may be hard. Just crank through as many as you can.
2. You must move quickly on the test, so practice answering questions quickly. Focus.
3. Correct your work. Study your errors. These are the errors you're most likely to make on the test. Now you know what they are so you can avoid making them when it counts.

Pomodoro 3: Tackle as many hard questions as you can.

1. Don't stress if they're too hard. You must keep moving. If you can't solve a hard question, circle it and come back later if there's time.
2. Correct your work. Study your errors.
3. Still can't figure out one or more questions? Don't let it eat up your study time. Either let it go or ask the teacher for help before class.

Pomodoro 4: Tackle as many easy questions as you can.

1. You can't afford mistakes on easy questions. You can't afford to waste time on easy questions. Practice that here: no mistakes, no wasted time.
2. You need enough time to answer medium and hard questions, so be fast and accurate on easy questions.
3. Correct your work. Study your errors. Don't make the same mistakes on easy questions on the test!

If you have more than two hours before your test, repeat the above plan for every two hours you have to study. If you have four hours, do it twice. If you need more time on hard questions and less time on easy questions, adjust accordingly. Don't end on the hard questions though. Trust me: Never end on hard questions! That can mess with your head and stress you out.

Now, you might be thinking, what if I try my hardest and fail anyway? I'm not gonna lie here. If you're unprepared now, you might fail tomorrow. You might fail your class. You might get grounded. You might not get into your dream college, if it's one of those places that likes kids who pass math. Failure sucks. It's disappointing. It's embarrassing. It makes you feel like you've wasted all your time and effort, while getting nothing in return. But let's be honest here. If you're doing this all the night before your test, you're not really wasting all that much time and effort. It's really just one night's worth of time and effort. You can bounce back from that, right?

Following are three secrets that A math students understand about failure. They're also secrets that Navy Seals, Olympians, and billionaires understand about failure:

- After you fail, you pick yourself up.
- After you fail, you learn from it.
- Most failures aren't as bad as being eaten by a bear.

So tomorrow, after the test, you'll pick yourself up and take inventory of what happened. What worked? What didn't? What will you do the same next time? What will you do differently?

Today, however, you study. Tonight, you study. You'll try your hardest because that's what champions do. In the big scheme of things, your math test is less like a bear and more like a raccoon. It looks scary and might leave a few scratches, but it won't actually kill you. Win or lose, you will wake up tomorrow, learn from your mistakes, and focus on a new day.

CRUSH MATH NOW

If your test is tomorrow, create a game plan to prepare for your test, then get studying.

GET SLEEP

Last but not least, the night before your test, you must get a good night's sleep! Don't study like crazy and then waste it all because you didn't get a good night's sleep. While I'll argue that the studying part is more important than the sleep part, sleep is still a close second. I'll tell you why:

Sleep improves your memory. And you'll need to be able to remember everything you studied for the test. I've been there—totally exhausted and staring at questions I know I reviewed the night before, but I'm too darn tired to remember what I need to do. Don't be the exhausted version of me that could've done better. Be smarter than that, and get some sleep. Consider sleeping to be part of your study plan, because it'll gain you a few points when you remember that one random formula on the test!

Sleep makes you more creative. Creativity solves problems. You'll need creative thinking when it comes to solving those hardest test questions. Consider sleep part of your study plan, because it'll gain you a few points—when you creatively find that one random solution to that one weird problem.

Sleep helps you focus. Students who are sleep-deprived tend to be inattentive and lose their train of thought. It's best to be hyper-focused on your test rather than having mush for a brain. Consider sleep part of your study plan, because it'll gain you a few points—by helping you finish the test faster...meaning you either will finish on time or have a few extra minutes to review your work and catch a mistake.

Sleep helps you avoid mistakes. The worst thing that can happen is that you know how to solve a problem but make a stupid mistake. Oh, how I hate that! The more tired you are, the more errors you'll make. This is the last time I'll say it: Consider sleeping to be part of your study plan, because it'll gain you a few points—by reducing errors.

Now, if you're one of those students who stress out and can't sleep the night before their test, here are a few tips for falling asleep.

Stick to a nighttime routine. The advice experts give parents to get their toddlers to sleep is the same advice I give grown math students. Have a set bedtime routine and morning routine. If things are routine, your brain goes on autopilot, knows what to do, and relaxes, making it easier to fall asleep. Find a good routine *before the night before the test* if possible, so you're already in the routine the night before the test.

No electronics after 8 pm. Screen time, whether it be your phone, computer, or TV, hinders falling asleep. During the last half hour to one hour before bed, don't try to relax by watching TV or checking your phone. Instead, read something positive and motivating—in paper form. I pick books that are good for me, but not so exciting that they'll keep me up all night. *The 7 Habits of Highly Effective People* by Stephen Covey or *Seven Strategies for Wealth and Happiness* by Jim Rohn are both books that are filled with advice to help you succeed in both math and life, but they aren't so exciting that you'll be up all night reading them.

Try rain music or vacuum cleaner sounds. Some people fall asleep better with these. I like the Relaxed Guy on YouTube. My kids like vacuum sounds. My middle kid likes rain music combined with piano—I can't stand it, but what works for one person doesn't necessarily work for the next! If you have trouble falling asleep, give a few different options a try. You'll either love something or hate it—but if you love it and it helps you fall asleep, it'll be worth it.

If you're a night owl or just too busy to get to bed on time, but it's affecting your math grade, make a commitment to change this. If you were too tired to do well on your last math test, then getting a good night's sleep is an integral part of preparing for your next test.

THINGS TO DO RIGHT BEFORE YOUR MATH TEST

Most students waste those few free minutes they have right before their test starts. Maybe the bell has not rung yet, or maybe the teacher is taking attendance or answering last-minute questions. Instead of wasting that time zoning out, or worse—talking to the unprepared student next to you, or getting freaked out, use the time you have right before the test starts to your advantage.

First, review anything you might forget. This is helpful no matter who you are. Review formulas, definitions, or a specific problem with multiple steps you might forget. This is especially important if you tried to cram all your memorizing into the night before because you forget a lot overnight. Review all those terms again right before your test. Refresh your memory.

Second, if you find yourself getting nervous right before the test or wishing you had studied more, here are a few proven strategies to help you deal with the fears. These are not strategies to eliminate your fears. Ultimately, you have to get through the math on the test while having those fears, but these strategies can help you perform better when you have test anxiety. I've had some students work through all five of these warm-up strategies and other students use just one or two. My suggestion is to try whatever you have time for. If it works, great! If not, try the next one. I had my Pre-algebra class do all five of these at the start of class for a month, and everyone found something that was helpful. It's just a matter of finding the one that's the most helpful for you.

Meditate. Take a minute to take some deep breaths. Concentrate your thoughts on your breathing, instead of the test. Just breathe. It seems like a silly strategy, but the students who find it helpful say it helps them forget about everything else in their lives, gives them confidence, and allows them to focus on math.

Write about your fears. A study completed by the University of Chicago and published in *Science* magazine showed that students with test anxiety did significantly better if they wrote about their testing fears right before a test, rather than simply trying to ignore their fears and power through. A few of my students really liked this strategy also. Writing down their fears acknowledged those fears, got them out of their head, and in turn allowed the students to focus on the math at hand.

Do warm-up questions. Starting a test by blanking out on an easy question sucks. It messes with your confidence for the whole rest of the test, so you want to make sure that you can confidently answer those first couple of easy questions on the test. To ensure that you can do this, do a couple of warm-up questions (i.e., easy and medium questions that you know the answers to). Just like you'd warm up your body before a soccer game or track meet, warming up your brain a little before test time will get you ready to go.

Remind yourself of your goals. If you're that student who gives up too easily and leaves questions blank on the test, then you need something that motivates you to keep working when the questions get tough. If you just give up on those harder test questions, remind yourself why you're here, why you're putting yourself through this torture of taking a math test. Take a minute to complete the following sentence: "I am committed to [goal] because [why it's important]." For example, "I'm committed to getting an A in math because then I can transfer to the college of my dreams, major in the subject that I really want to major in, go on to get my dream job, and live the life of my dreams." Another example would be, "I'm committed to getting an A in math because I want to be the kind of person who can do hard things, overcome any challenge, and crush anything." The feedback I get on this particular exercise is that it helps students power through their test when they'd normally just give up and leave problems blank. (The feedback for doing this on a daily basis is that it helps them show up to class more often and complete more of their homework—according to my slacker students.)

Visualize the math. This is something I've always done. As a student, I thought this was slacker studying because I was too busy to actually redo problems to study for tests, so I'd just look at them and *think* about what I'd do. I'd think through each step without actually doing it. I never realized there was a name for this until I was reading about how Olympic athletes use a technique called visualization. They visualize their race or game or whatever it is they're going to do before they actually do it. They can see, hear, feel, and experience exactly what they're going to go through before they actually do it. This is exactly how I would warm up for a test. I would skim through problems in my notes and think about the steps. I thought it was a quick hack to make up for being unprepared right before a test, but as it turns out, it's a well-known tool that the most successful people in the world use intentionally.

There are other things I've had students experiment with immediately before a test, but the methods above are the ones that my students have found the most helpful. If none of them seem to give you an extra edge on your test, brainstorm nine other things that you could do right before your test that would help you, and try those instead. It doesn't matter what specific tactical strategy you use right before your test. What's important is that you use those few minutes before your test to your advantage and do something that helps you.

CRUSH MATH NOW

Create a quick practice quiz with hard problems. Use one of the methods above *immediately before* you take the practice quiz. Did it help? Were you able to answer the hard questions correctly if you used one of the above methods right before starting your quiz? Experiment until you find a method that works.

TEST-TAKING STRATEGIES FOR DURING YOUR TEST

If math class is equivalent to soccer practice, then math homework is equivalent practicing soccer on your own, math tests are equivalent to soccer games, and your final exam is basically the championship game, should you make it that far. Everything in the soccer season has been to prepare you for that championship game. Likewise, everything in your math semester is to prepare you for your final exam. Ideally, your soccer team will try out different game plans in varying sequences during games throughout the season, so by the time they get to the championship game, they know exactly what works and what doesn't. Likewise, you should try out different test-taking strategies on the quizzes and tests leading up to your final exam so by the time you get to your final, you know exactly what works and what doesn't. Here are my favorite test-taking strategies for you to use during your next quiz, test, or final exam.

Write down anything you might forget as soon as you get the test. If there's a rule, formula, or definition you might forget in the middle of the test, write it down the second you get your test. Even before you read the directions. In Trigonometry, there were a bunch of trig identities that we had to know. A bunch! It was terrible. My teacher would say we shouldn't need to memorize them because we should under-stand where the equations were derived from. Blah, blah, blah. In retrospect, she was totally right, but at the time, I thought trig functions were stupid and pointless and as far removed from real life as math could get. I couldn't care less about understanding them. I just cared about the grade, so I crammed my memorization in the night before the test, reviewed the equations again right before the test, and wrote the equations down *the second I got the test*. Smartest test-taking strategy ever, as I was able to crush Trigonometry without fully appreciating the depths of how beautiful trig functions can be.

Read the directions! I cannot articulate how bonkers this makes me when students lose points just because they forgot to read the directions! Do you get penalized more for wrong answers than omitted answers? Can there be more than one correct answer? Can you get partial credit for showing work? Are you allowed to use your calculators, or will pulling out your calculator get you kicked out of the test? Do you need to grid your answers in with a number two pencil? We put directions like this on the test not because we enjoy torturing you with pointless, arbitrary rules. We put these directions on the test because the archaic scantron reader doesn't pick up anything besides number two pencils! If the test says to show your work, it's so we can give you partial credit when half the class inevitably screws up on that one problem that everyone screws up on year after year after year. Read the directions! (And then follow them.)

Skim through the test. Glance over the whole test so you know what you're up against and can make sure you're working at a pace that will give you enough time to finish the test. As you skim through problems, also jot down notes about anything you think you might forget. Five students on the last midterm I gave didn't finish the test. Three did phenomenal on the questions they actually answered, but they didn't pace themselves correctly and ran out of time. Believe me, it pained me to pry the test from their fingers, but when the test is done, it's done. All that heartache, all of those lost points, could have been saved if they'd skimmed through the test to see where the difficult problems were and paced themselves appropriately.

Keep a strong pace on easy and medium questions. Students have a tendency to mistakenly think that the first 50 percent of the test questions should take 50 percent of the time on the test. This is not always the case. On my last Statistics quiz, there were twenty questions. The first ten consisted of quick definitions and simple calculations and should have taken only 10 percent of the time allotted for the test. The last ten questions were hard word problems that required both a lot of thought and many calculations. These should have taken 90 percent of the time allotted for the test, and those students who meandered through the first half ended up not finishing the second half.

Circle and come back to hard questions. If you find that a question is taking a lot of time, come back to it. Unless your test is on a computer that requires you to answer questions in order, you do not have to answer the questions on your test in sequential order, and there are always a few harder questions on every test. Teachers design it this way. There are always one or two questions that are harder than the rest; we put those in to differentiate between the students who deserve 90 percent on the test and those who deserve 100 percent. Only those select few, strong A students will get them right. If 100 percent isn't your goal, then circle these questions. Even if they're the first two questions on the test or right smack in the middle of the test, skip them, answer everything else first, then come back and tackle them last.

Ask your teacher questions. Don't ask, "Is this right?" or "What is the quadratic formula?" or even "How do I do this?" Ask questions your teacher is actually able to answer. When directions or phrasing in a question are unclear, ask what we mean. When there are things that don't make sense, ask about it. When I was a student, my Calculus teacher gave us a multiple-choice final exam, where three questions had answers, none of which were correct. Thank goodness somebody asked! This last semester, I accidentally game my Statistics class a quiz with a question asking about "standard variation"—a confusing, vague combination of words similar to those we'd studied— when I meant to write "standard deviation," a term we'd spent weeks studying. Again, thank goodness somebody asked about it.

Guess. If you don't know the answer or even where to start, force yourself to write something down. Even if you have no idea, take a guess that's related to what you were studying in the current chapter or semester. What was the first step you took or formula you used in your homework problems? Look for any keywords or hints, and start there. An unanswered question is a guaranteed zero points. Nothing can be worse than that. When I took Number Theory, I was positive I'd failed my first exam. I guessed on every single question on the test, wrote total guesses based upon the material we'd covered in class, and walked away feeling like a moron. When I went to ask my professor if he thought I should drop the class, he told me I had scored a B+ on the exam. He'd designed the exam to be hard and to force us to work through problems that we couldn't possibly get through. The fact that I tried and tried and tried, despite how hopeless and moronic I was feeling, had saved me. The fact that my guesses were grounded in the concepts we'd learned in class, saved me. There are countless other math classes I've taken where this technique has similarly paid off. They say in life that 90 percent of success is showing up. I swear the other 10 percent is just trying when you're there. If you don't know, guess. Always.

Re-read the question. Word problems are the hardest! On a Statistics quiz I gave my class, several questions asked students to find the probability of something happening. Most of the work for these questions revolved around finding the number of possible outcomes, and the very last step required using that number to find the probability. Some students obviously knew how to do every single step and showed that work clearly, but because they forgot to re-read the question, they forgot to do that last simple step and got the question wrong. Hard SAT Math questions are intentionally designed this way to trip up students who forget to re-read the question. Multiple-choice questions typically have a wrong answer choice that is the answer you'd get if you forgot to re-read the question. Don't miss points for something as simple as re-reading the question on word problems. Always re-read the question!

Estimate or think about what makes sense. Is your answer reasonable, or did you wind up with some wonky, totally illogical answer? Should your answer be a tiny fraction or a number in the thousands? If the math you work through gives you an answer that is unlikely, illogical or crazy, it's probably wrong and you should check your work. As I'm writing this chapter, I'm reflecting on last week's Statistics quiz and telling you all the things I hope my students remember for next week's midterm. Last week's quiz had questions about the probability of something happening. Probabilities must be between zero and one. If you got anything else, you know it must be a mistake, yet students answered -7, 1.4, and a number in the hundreds. Come on, people! Think about whether your answer makes sense!

CRUSH MATH NOW

Each soccer season, the game plan I have for my team for the first soccer game is always the worst, but I have to start somewhere. As a coach with a new team, I make my best guess as to where players should play, give it a shot, learn from my mistakes and improve from there.

In your *Crush Math Now Game Plan*, create a game plan for the night before, right before and during your next math test. Add any strategies from this chapter that could potentially be high-impact on your next exam. Don't worry if it's not perfect. Just make your best guess and go for it.

11. OPTIMIZE WHAT YOU'RE DOING

Kevin wanted a perfect SAT score, so he took a practice SAT test, meaning he sat down for four full hours and took an entire SAT test from beginning to end. The SAT was as an important test that would determine where he went to college, so he didn't mind giving up half his Saturday. He did really well and only missed two questions, but he wanted a perfect score. He took another practice test, giving up four more hours on another Saturday, hoping to improve. He missed two questions again, so he took another practice test. He still missed two questions, so he took yet another practice test. He repeated this twenty-four times and still missed one or two questions each time. Twenty-four Saturdays wasted. Nearly 100 hours wasted. All that pain and stress and trying really hard, and for what? To be further from a perfect SAT score because now be believed he was incapable of getting a perfect score.

Priscilla, my student with test anxiety from Chapter 1, studied really hard for her first College Precalculus test. It was an important class, the one that was standing between her and her dream of going to nursing school, so she didn't mind studying so much. She tried really hard and studied really hard, but she failed her test anyway. She didn't give up though, because she's not the kind of student who just gives up on her dreams. She buckled down and studied even more for her next Precalculus test, but she failed that one, too. Now, it was the end of the semester, and her final exam would determine whether or not she passed College Precalculus. She studied every single day for a week, hours upon hours, days upon days, but still failed her final exam and, therefore, the class. She was now wrought with test anxiety, but she didn't give up. She took the class two more times, studying longer and harder with each test, developing more and more extreme test anxiety with each test. She failed the class the second time and withdrew the third. Three semesters wasted. A year and a half wasted. Thousands of hours wasted. All that pain and stress and trying really hard, and for what? To be further away from her dreams than when she started.

A few years ago, I was diagnosed with a form of cancer that required both surgery and chemotherapy. After the surgery, when I was cleared to start exercising again, I jumped right in, excited to run my first post-cancer half marathon, but the result was excruciating pain in my abdomen on par with when my epidural wore off during labor. The pain scared me, but I'm not one to give up easily, and I wanted to run another half marathon. So I took time off to recover and tried running again, this time more slowly and more scared of the pain. The result? Excruciating pain in my abdomen, so I took time off again to recover and tried again. And again. And again. This is how my last two years have been. Recover. Try running. Pain. Repeat. Two years wasted. Hundreds of hours wasted. All that physical pain endured. And for what? To be further away from my dream of running a half marathon because now just the idea of running gives me anxiety.

"Insanity is doing the same thing over and over and expecting different results," says Albert Einstein, according to the Internet. Don't make the same mistake that Kevin made, that Priscilla made, or that I made.

Don't waste weeks or years making little changes that have no impact. If you've been struggling with math (or any problem) for an extended period of time, I want you to write this quote down somewhere you will see it often:

**Insanity is doing the same thing
over and over
and expecting different results.**

Don't be insane. Don't waste hours upon hours. Don't waste semesters upon semesters. Don't waste all your energy and hope and confidence making tiny, trivial changes. Go big or go home.

How? There are many ways, but the two that work the most consistently are tracking and the Rule of Nine. First, let's talk about tracking.

TRACK YOUR PROGRESS

You should always know what you've done, what you've accomplished, and what you have yet to do. On a paper, create two columns; label one *High-Impact* and the other *Low-Impact*. As you try different strategies, add them to the column in which they belong. As you see the lists grow, you'll see the hard work you've put in, how many different strategies you've tried, and which ones are having a positive impact on your grade. It doesn't matter how you track your progress, but you must find some way that's simple and enables you to see which strategies are *High-Impact*.

Whenever you learn something new, it's important to experiment and track. For this book, for example, everything I'm doing is something new I'm learning, so I'm tracking things, too. For writing, I keep a list of writing strategies and techniques, try them out, and track their usefulness. For marketing the book, I'll do something similar. For tracking the effectiveness of the book, I will use Amazon reviews. The more reviews I have, the more I know the book has reached students and the more five-star reviews it has, the more impact I know it's having on students. (Hint, please let me know whether *Crush Math Now* helped you by leaving me an honest review!) Just like how your game plan for crushing math is a rough draft right now, something that will get better every day, this book is the same. I will try different things. I will track the results. I will learn from my mistakes and improve. Remember, mistakes are not something to be afraid of. Mistakes are proof that you're trying something new, something challenging, and something worthwhile. Learning from mistakes is vital to growing and making Future You more awesome.

THE RULE OF NINE

Combining tracking with the Rule of Nine is what will enable you to optimize how you're crushing math. In a screenwriting class, I learned this cool tool that comedy writers use. When writing a joke, they come up with nine different endings and choose the funniest. It turns out that the funniest isn't always first or second or even third. Sometimes, it's the eighth or ninth option that you really struggle to find. This rule works for identifying problems and solutions as well.

Eventually, after twenty-four practice SAT tests, Kevin's parents hired me, as a tutor, to help him out. What did I do? I had him brainstorm nine ways to prepare for the SAT differently. Nine. Why? Because without forcing yourself to brainstorm different solutions, you'll always go with the most familiar way. In Kevin's case, the most familiar way had been to repeat taking practice test after practice test after practice test. His list of nine solutions looked like this:

1. Take another four-hour practice test. (Ugh!)
2. Review the incorrect questions to see what the careless errors are.
3. Review more SAT questions.
4. Solve more SAT questions.
5. Solve more SAT questions and practice checking for errors.
6. Solve more SAT questions and make a list of all careless errors or mistakes made.
7. Solve more *hard* SAT questions.
8. Review the questions he got right on the test, so he knew what he didn't need to study.
9. Read up on SAT strategies for hard questions.

Next, I asked Kevin which solutions will be the most impactful. There were so many options that were more impactful than taking another four-hour practice test! Kevin decided on number two: *Review the incorrect questions to see what the careless errors were.* (By the way, this should always be the very first thing you do after a quiz, test or practice test.) Then, he combined numbers five, six, and seven: *Solve more hard SAT questions and practice checking for errors. Then, make a list of all careless errors and mistakes made.* Now that is an effective study plan! The fact that he first took twenty-four four-hour practice tests without ever reviewing his mistakes pains me!

Don't be like Kevin, taking the insane route to not

getting a perfect SAT score. Don't be like Priscilla, taking the insane route to failing College Precalculus. Don't be like me, taking the insane route to not being able to run a marathon. Each of us had a big, hairy, audacious goal (BHAG). Each of us had motivation, discipline, grit, and a village to support us, but each of us struggled to reach our goals because we were not focusing on big, high-impact changes or consistently analyzing what we were doing to reach our goals. Instead of being like Kevin, Priscilla, and me, use the Rule of Nine to optimize your game plan for crushing math.

CRUSH MATH NOW

This is the final *Crush Math Now* assignment in this book. It is the biggest one, the longest one, and the hardest one. It is the one that will take days instead of minutes. It's the one that requires brutally honest self-assessment and forcing yourself out of your comfort zone. It is the assignment that will pull all the pieces from this book together to enable you to crush math. It is the assignment you can come back to whenever you need to get yourself back on track. It includes the steps throughout the book that you must take to optimize your game plan enough to ultimately reach your goals.

Ready?

Here it goes:

1. **Create the rough draft of your game plan.** If you haven't already, get some paper or open up a document on your computer. Write *Crush Math Now Game Plan* across the top, then do all the exercises from Chapter 2 here. You now have your three obstacles (your grades, your competency, and you),

your goals, and a rough draft of everything you will do to achieve your goals in one place.

2. **Learn from your mistakes.** On paper, create two lists: *Don't Know It* and *Know It*. Review your last quiz, test, or practice quiz. Add every mistake you made to the *Don't Know It* list. Add everything you know well and don't need to waste time studying to the *Know It* list.

3. **Use the Rule of Nine.** Brainstorm and write down nine high-impact strategies to prepare for your next quiz or test.

4. **Focus on Now:** Pick the strategies that you think will be the most impactful and do them *now*. Don't go for the easiest. Get out of your comfort zone— the fastest progress is often made doing the things we're hesitant to try.

5. **Track Your Progress:** Create two more lists, one titled *High-Impact* and the other titled *Low-Impact*. As you try out strategies from *Crush Math Now*, add each strategy to one of the lists. If it's high-impact, continue using it. If it's not, can you tweak it or do you need to lose it?

6. **Repeat** until you meet your goals.

Do this frequently when you're first making changes. Hourly, if you want to see improvement over the course of a day or weekend. Daily, to see improvement over the course of a week. Weekly, if you want to see improvement over the course of a month. After that, do this after every quiz or test for general grade maintenance.

If done quickly and repeatedly, you can make more changes in a short time than many students make over the course of their entire education. You can go from failing math to crushing it in a week or a weekend. Then, by repeating the steps after every quiz and test, you can maintain being a math-crushing student for the remainder of your education.

IN CONCLUSION

There you have it, the big stuff, the high-impact strategies I've used over the last two decades to help my students crush math. Every hack to study faster and, in turn, take tests faster. Every strategy to learn the material in greater depth. Every resource you have at your disposal. Every trick, hack, or strategy for gaining the most points on exams. Every "pick yourself up when you fall" story I've given disheartened students. Every "toughen-up" speech I've given lazy students. Every lesson you can learn from my own experiences and the experiences of my students. I hope that something, some-where in this book is that hidden gem, that missing link, that you needed to crush math.

The very last thought I'd like to leave you with is this: Remember that the road to success in math, as well as in life, is not linear. It is not a straight line with simple, easy-to-follow directions guiding you each step of the way. The road to success in math, as well as in life, is chaotic. Embrace the chaos. Crush the chaos when you can. Pick yourself up when it crushes you. It is a constant, ever-changing battle to be fought.

There is a branch of mathematics called Chaos Theory that studies the constant, ever-changing chaos in complex systems. It says that complex systems, much like your journey to succeed in math and life, are highly sensitive to slight changes in conditions. This means that teeny, tiny changes can result in crazy, humongous consequences. My hope is that hidden somewhere in *Crush Math Now* is a teeny tiny change that, if made, will change the course of your life. I hope that it will give you the tools necessary to crush math. I hope that math will, in turn, empower you and teach you to solve your problems and conquer challenges. I hope that math will develop within you confidence, grit, and discipline. I hope that math will enable you to figure out how to do the things you think you cannot do so that you can live a bigger, bolder, more inspired life. I hope you will crush math today, so Future You can crush anything tomorrow.

Stephen King once wrote,

> **Get a little rock and roll on the radio**
> **and go toward all the life there is**
> **with all the courage you can find**
> **and all the belief you can muster.**

Life is short, and I encourage you to go that extra mile, live life to the fullest, and be the best that you can be. And the best version of yourself, no matter who you are, is someone who is capable of crushing math.

A QUICK FAVOR

Thank you so much for reading *Crush Math Now*!

Will you take a moment to leave an honest review for this book on Amazon? My goal is to help as many students as possible to succeed in math and reviews are the *best* way to encourage others to purchase the book. Seriously, I can't tell you how much reviews help!

Thank you so much for your help! And thanks so much for reading! I appreciate you!

GRATITUDE

The kids, I hope so much that this book will leave your world a little better. I will love you to the last digit of pi.

Mom and Dad, for raising me to love math and soccer. Everything in this book that is tough, wise, or of value started with you.

Christy, for encouraging me to pursue a more creative life. It's been so fun taking the road less traveled with you.

The Uyeshimas, for being amazing teachers and coaches who have taught me so much over the years. Uncle Dave, thank you for encouraging me to volunteer to help your students with math. That experience has stayed with me always.

My Prealgebra students, for every time you tackle something big and bold. The sky's the limit and I am so excited to see all the amazing things you will accomplish.

My many inspiring math professors and teachers at Flintridge Sacred Heart Academy, Scripps College, and Claremont Graduate University: Mrs. Mikrut, Mr. Nishiyama, Sister Ramona, Prof. Towse, Prof. Chaderjian, Prof. Ou, Prof. Myhre, Prof. Angus and Prof. Nadim. Your classes not only teach, they inspire.

The many amazing professors at Irvine Valley College and Golden West College: Brent Monte, Joe Sheldon, Pete Bouser, JoAnne Noyes, Rich Zucker, Ilknur Erbas White, and Lan Phan. I have been blessed to have you as colleagues and mentors.

My friends, for helping me to make the most of each stage of my life.

My book team, Honoree Corder, Megan Haskell, Tammi Metzler, Dan Foster, and Jerald Anino. Without you, this would just be a long rant about math lost somewhere in Evernote.

ABOUT THE AUTHOR

Allison Dillard is a math professor at Irvine Valley College and an optimist who believes that anyone can crush math. She has an M.S. in Mathematics from Claremont Graduate University, where she was the recipient of fellowships from the National Science Foundation, Boeing, and Los Alamos National Lab. She has a B.A. in English and a B.A. in Mathematics from Scripps College, where she received the Reed Institute's award for "Excellence in Problem Analysis and Problem Solving in Decision Science." When she's not teaching or writing, you'll find her playing board games with her awesome husband, coaching her kids' soccer teams, or dreaming up new ways to convince the world that math is awesome. Her love for math is legendary.